Jonathan Holden is a Partner, Head of I
Education for Forbes Solicitors. He ha
ment Law throughout his career. Jonathan has extensive
experience in advising public sector institutions; and is a nationally recognised expert in advising on employment law issues
within the education sector.

He is an experienced Tribunal advocate, and regularly appears in
Employment Tribunals throughout the country. He is experienced in dealing with pension loss issues, and appeared in one of
the leading cases in this area in the Employment Appeals
Tribunal. Jonathan is one of few experts nationally on LGPS and
Teacher's Pension issues; and he is currently dealing with a Court
of Appeal case dealing with gross misconduct in the Education
sector. He commonly deals with complicated discrimination and
whistle-blowing cases. In addition, he is experienced in dealing
with both the non-contentious and contentious implications of
the Transfer of Undertakings (Protection of Employment) Regulations and advises clients on these issues both internally, and at
Tribunal if necessary.

In addition, Jonathan presents seminars to clients on all aspects of
Employment Law and provides bespoke in-house training to meet
client demand. He also regularly comments on Employment
issues to local media and radio as well writing for and on the
education sector; and has recently been retained by a national
training provider to train lawyers on employment law issues
within the education sector.

A Practical Guide to Advising Schools on Employment Law

A Practical Guide to Advising Schools on Employment Law

Jonathan J Holden
Solicitor

Law Brief Publishing

Published 2018 by Law Brief Publishing, an imprint of
Law Brief Publishing Ltd
30 The Parks
Minehead
Somerset
TA24 8BT

www.lawbriefpublishing.com

Paperback: 978-1-911035-71-8

For Malachy, Eirinn and Magnus:

this book, like everything I do,

is done for them.

PREFACE

The aim of this book is to assist those advising Schools on day-to-day employment law issues. Written from a legal perspective, the text will primarily be of use to lawyers, although I hope that School Business Managers, Bursars, Heads and Governors will find it of use too.

When I started acting on behalf of Schools some ten years' ago, I quickly found myself thrust into a world of acronyms, statutory guidance and rules which were at first unfamiliar. Although the law itself was similar, the setting and the context in which it was employed certainly created some significant differences. I hope that this text will assist those who, like me, found the task of becoming familiar with advising Schools to be a daunting task. Similarly, I hope that experienced practitioners will find it a useful source of go to information.

Rather than descend into mundane detail, I have focused on the most common areas of difficulty and peculiarity in advising the sector; looking at the tricky issues that come up for myself and my team on the most regular basis. There may be areas that readers would like to see covered either at all, or in more detail: please do feedback to me if that is the case, so that future editions can be enhanced and refined.

Although all my own work, this book would not have happened without the support of family, friends and colleagues for which I am eternally grateful. The law is correct as of February 2018, and all errors are my own. I welcome all feedback by your preferred medium, either email (jonathan.holden@forbessolicitors.co.uk) or Twitter (@jonathanjholden).

Jonathan Holden
February 2018

CONTENTS

CHAPTER ONE
WHO IS THE EMPLOYER?

Introduction

A key question for any employment practitioner; you could even say crucial – for how else do we know who to sue? But in the Education sector this is not always an easy question to answer. In this chapter we will examine both the different types of Schools within the sector, together with specific rules peculiar to the differing types. We will conclude with a look at the key provisions of the School Staffing (England) Regulations 2009; and the impact these Regulations have on advising Schools within the maintained sector.

Types of Schools

There are a dizzying array of different Schools within the education landscape; but all can be categorised into three main types:

- Academies (including multi-academy trusts);

- Maintained Schools; and

- Independent Schools

Within Academies, MATs and Independent Schools, identifying the correct Employer is relatively straightforward: the Employer will be the Academy Trust, or the organisation by which the independent school is owned or run.

Those with one eye on the future will note the increasing prevalence of multi-academy trusts, in particular, (though this point applies equally to stand-alone academies) being set up as charitable institutions: bringing with it the extra layer of regulatory oversight provided by the Charity Commission.

In a maintained School, the position as to who the correct Employer is can be confusing. It is not unknown for maintained Schools themselves to be confused and/or incorrect. My advice and standard practice is always where possible to obtain the up-to-date OFSTED[1] report to verify the information provided on instructions: this provides the type of School within the section headed 'School Details' towards the end of the report.

Furthermore, although the position is improving, Tribunal Judges (and opponents, for that matter) can also find the situation confusing. This can particularly be the case when, for example, the correct Employer is the governing body of a maintained School; but the award can be enforced against the relevant local authority: as in the case of a Community School with a delegated budget.

I can do no better than re-produce the table that proudly adorns our office wall to assist us in identifying the correct employer in the maintained sector:

---

1   The weblink being: https://reports.ofsted.gov.uk

Type of School	Employer	Statutory Reference
Community	Local Authority	s.35 Education Act 2002
Community w/delegated budget	Respondent is governing body (awards enforceable against LA)	Education (Modification of Enactments Relating to Employment) Orders
Community Special	Local Authority	s.35 Education Act 2002
Community Special w/delegated budget	Respondent is governing body (awards enforceable against LA)	Education (Modification of Enactments Relating to Employment) Orders
Voluntary Controlled	Local Authority	s.35 Education Act 2002
Voluntary Controlled w/delegated budget	Respondent is governing body (awards enforceable against LA)	Education (Modification of Enactments Relating to Employment) Orders
Foundation	Governing Body	s.36 Education Act 2002
Foundation Special	Governing Body	s.36 Education Act 2002
Voluntary Aided	Governing Body	s.36 Education Act 2002

Those Employees who have been employed at a voluntary-aided School since before 1996 will retain the Local Authority, rather than the Governing Body, as their Employer.

Aside from an academic point of interest, why does all this matter? Unfortunately, different regimes apply to different types of School, dependent on the type of School. This is particularly the case in the areas of appointment and dismissal. The overarching framework is laid out in the School Staffing (England Regulations) 2009, the important features of which are detailed below. Note also the existence of The Staffing of Maintained Schools (Wales) Regulations 2006: although largely in similar terms to their English counterparts, there are some differences, which fall outside the scope of this work.

School Staffing Regulations

These Regulations apply to maintained Schools within the sectors. The Staffing Regulations divide themselves into three main sections:

Part 1 – General (i.e. Provisions relevant to all maintained Schools);

Part 2 – Provisions relating to Community, Voluntary Controlled, Community Special and Maintained Nursery Schools (i.e. those Schools where the local authority is the Employer);

Part 3 – Provisions relating to Foundation, Voluntary Aided and Foundation Special Schools (i.e. those Schools where the Governing Body is the Employer).

Part 1 confirms (Regulation 7) that it is the responsibility of the Governing Body to establish disciplinary and grievance procedures. Even though they may in practice adopt the local authority procedures, a note of this adoption (and the adoption of subsequent amendments and alterations) ought to be made within the minutes of the governing body meeting that confirms this. Similarly, note here there is no *obligation* on the School to adopt the local authority procedures. However, in the case of all maintained Schools, Regulation 6 provides the Local Authority with the power to make written representations to the governing body in the event of *'serious concerns'* as to the performance of the head teacher. A copy must be sent to the head teacher, and the governing body are required to notify the authority of the action they propose to take in light of the report.

Regulation 8 requires the governing body to establish capability procedures; and Regulation 8A confirms that if a request is received from another School as to whether a former member of staff had been the subject of capability procedures in the last two years, the governing body must provide written details to that subsequent School.

Regulation 8A should therefore be considered in the drafting, or advising on, any settlement agreement involving staff at a maintained school. As a statutory obligation, a school ought not to be derogating from this responsibility, and it is important to consider this when, for example, agreeing an agreed form of reference.

This Regulation can also help when advising an employer faced with an obviously agreed reference appearing to emanate from a settlement agreement. If this is the case, and the former employer is a maintained school, the employer could make a written request pursuant to Regulation 8A: it may produce no result, but could avoid the potential hire of an undesirable employee who might otherwise appear acceptable on the face of an agreed reference.

The Regulations contain specific requirements for the appointment of staff members at various levels. Experience dictates that this rarely become an issue for practitioners, so it is outside the scope of this work to go into the mundane detail set out on this.

In Schools where the Local Authority is the ultimate employer (Community, Voluntary Controlled, Community Special and Maintained Nursery Schools), Regulation 19 applies to suspension. This confirms that the governing body or the head teacher has the power to suspend staff, but must notify the Authority immediately of the suspension. Only a governing body can end the suspension, and the governing body must immediately inform the authority and the head of the ending of the suspension. Regulation 19 specifically prohibits suspension without pay.

Where the Governing Body is the employer (Foundation, Voluntary Aided and Foundation Special Schools), unless the staff in question are employed by the authority, the same provisions apply, save that there is no requirement to notify the authority. Again, only the governing body may end a suspension, and suspension without pay is prohibited (Regulation 31).

In *Birmingham City Council v. Emery [2014] ELR 203*, a case dealing with a Community School (in which the Local Authority is the Employer), the Employment Appeals Tribunal looked at the provisions of Regulation 20 of the School Staffing (England) Regulations 2009, which state:

"Dismissal of staff:

(1)   *Subject to Regulation 21, where the governing body determines that any person employed or engaged by the authority to work at the school should cease to work there, it must notice the authority in writing of its determination and the reasons for it.*

(2)   *If the person concerned in employed or engaged to work solely at the school (and does not resign), the authority must, before the end of the period of fourteen days beginning with the date of the notification under paragraph (1), either-*

a. *Terminate the person's contract with the authority, giving such notice as is required under that contract; or*

b. *Terminate such contract without notice if the circumstances are such that it is entitled to do so by reason of the person's conduct.*

(3)   *If the person concerned is not employed or engaged by the authority to work solely at the school, the authority must require the person to cease to work at the school"*[2]

Ms Emery was employed as a teacher at the school under a contract of employment. Her contract of employment provided for termination with two months' notice expiring on the 30th April or with four months' notice expiring on the 31st August but not on any date in between. Because the school was a community school, the local authority was her employer, Regulation 20 provided that if the governing body determined that she should be dismissed, her employment had to be terminated by the authority.

_____

2   Regulation 20, School Staffing (England) Regulations 2009, SI 2009/2680

On February 28, a meeting of a panel of governors (which was attended by a representative of the local authority) determined that Ms Emery ought to be dismissed. The local authority representative stated that the date of dismissal was the date of the meeting; that she was entitled to contractual notice pay, ending 30th April, and that a letter confirming the dismissal would be sent to her. Whilst the governing body wrote to her on the 28th February, confirming that the local authority would be terminating her contract on notice ending April 30; it was not until the 29th February that the local authority wrote to her formally terminating her employment as of the 30th April. Ms Emery did not receive the letter until the 1st March. In the employment tribunal, the Judge concluded that the letter was one day too late to give her the notice to which she was contractually entitled and awarded her a further four months' pay.

Although the Authority argued that the employment had been ended by either the governing body or the representative of the local authority at the meeting on the 28th February, that was not accepted by the EAT. The letters produced specifically countermanded that view. Furthermore, it was accepted by the EAT that the Regulations to not permit a delegation by a local authority of what is their statutory obligation imposed by Regulation 20.

There is an interesting aspect to the Regulations cited: the authority clearly has some limited decision-making role; and the authority has to carry out its statutory duty. If they fail to do so, either on time (the authority has 14 days), or at all, this can have a serious effect on the Employees.

Regulation 20 does not on the face of things give the authority an option: they *must* terminate the employment within 14 days either with or without notice as the case dictates. I would always advise checking this point, particularly if running an unfair dismissal case for a member of School staff: it may turn out they may not have been dismissed at all; for example, if the authority has overlooked confirming the dismissal.

I would also bear in mind the effect of the recent decision of the Court of Appeal in *Haywood v. Newcastle upon Tyne [2017] EWCA Civ 153* which has a bearing on this situation. In that case, the Employee was sent a letter by recorded delivery on the 20th April: notifying her that she was dismissed by reason of redundancy and providing 12 weeks' notice. At the time, she was on holiday; and in the event she did not read the letter until the 27th April. At issue was the actual date of dismissal: specifically, whether this was before or after the Employee's 50th birthday, which had a bearing on her pension entitlement. The Court agreed that the contents of the letter had to be communicated to the Employee before it took effect: and in this case that was the 27th April, so that the employment was not terminated until after the Employee's 50th birthday.

This can obviously have a significant bearing within the Education sector: not only since most (if not all) Employees will be members of either the Teacher's Pension Scheme or the Local Government Pension Scheme – both of which have distinct age related benefits (for example, in the case of redundancy); and due to the specific notice periods for teachers in the maintained sector provided by the Burgundy Book.

In *Davies v. Haringey LBC [2014] EWHC 3393 (QB)* the Claimant, a full-time trade union representative ostensibly employed at a Community School argued that the Local Authority had no power to suspend and/or discipline her. Although not the only reason that forms part of the ratio of the case, nevertheless the High Court accepted that the School Staffing (England) Regulations 2009 were sufficiently drafted so as to allow the Local Authority to suspend and discipline the Claimant; utilising the Local Authorities disciplinary procedures rather than those of the School. The Claimant had been released for the last 14 years of her employment and then suspended pursuant to an allegation that she had breached the authority's Code of Conduct and Social Media Policy: the allegations were unrelated to her teaching. Her argument that both the School Staffing Regulations and the Education (Modification of Enactments Relating to Employment) (England) Order 2003 (the "Modification Order") effectively meant that the material employment powers were held exclusively by the School was unsuccessful. The Judge in that case interpreted Regulation 19 of the School Staffing (England) Regulations (which deals with the suspension of staff) as not granting *exclusive* power to the governing body or Head teacher to suspend; and also confirmed that the Modification Order has no bearing on the parties' contractual rights.

This principle could be particularly useful for any local authority faced with a similar situation: or for a small School without the resources to conduct a thorough investigation; or, for example, in the case of the Employee in question having some sort of conflict with the governing body. Wherever it is employed, good practice would be to produce a formal note of the proposed course of action at the relevant meeting of the governing body, or subcommittee, as the case may be. It is also important to ensure that the Employee understands the process to be adopted to avoid a potential finding of procedurally unfair dismissal.

Identity of the correct Employer of course makes a difference in the drafting of pleadings: but consider also the effect in drafting settlement agreements. A drafting error here could well lead to a negligence claim. My own preference in any case where the Employer is ultimately the Local Authority is to include both the Local Authority and the local governing body as parties to the agreement: thus being both 'bullet-proof'; and also settling any potential standalone case of discrimination against the governing body. This is of course only possible where one is instructed by both the Local Authority and the governing body.

Summary

As can be seen, identity of the correct employer when advising any School is crucially important. Practitioners should take care in naming the correct Respondent in Tribunal or Court proceedings, and for those that represent Respondents, to correct errors in this respect. An audit of the processes adopted within the maintained sector, particularly around suspension and dismissal, is also important given the restrictive provisions of the School Staffing (England) Regulations. As ever, the paper trail will be crucial, and there are certainly traps for the unwary or unexperienced practitioner to be aware of.

CHAPTER TWO
TERMS AND CONDITIONS

Introduction

There are a number of unique factors in relation to terms and conditions to be aware of when advising in the sector. Within this chapter we will look at the important points arising from the following:

- The School Teachers' Pay and Conditions Document ("STPCD")

- The Burgundy Book

- The Green Book

- Points specific to Independent Schools and Academies

- The effect of the Modification Order on the sector

- Pensions Issues

The aim of this chapter is to provide an overview of the most common issues arising within the sector, providing practitioners with an easy point of reference for most issues; whilst not undermining the importance of reviewing the relevant source material where necessary.

School Teachers' Pay and Conditions Document

The principal source of terms and conditions for employed teachers remains the statutory School Teachers' Pay and Conditions Document ("STPCD"), which is updated annually.

STPCD remains relevant for most (if not all) academies, the vast majority choosing to adopt this document as the terms and conditions of employment at least initially on transfer (as of course TUPE prescribes they must do); and thereafter.

STPCD sets out the pay regime for both teachers and senior leaders in Schools; including the requirement for performance related pay, which is dealt with in the chapter on performance management. The document also sets out the contractual framework for teachers at differing levels, including professional responsibilities of both teacher and head teachers; as well as working time requirements: in particular, the requirement to be available for work for 1265 hours or a pro-rata equivalent for part-time staff.

The overriding responsibilities set out in Part 7 are particularly useful when advising on performance management and/or misconduct issues; setting out core responsibilities to which reference can be made when dealing with such issues. Part 7 sets out specific professional responsibilities for Head teachers, Deputies, and ordinary teachers. In the case of a disciplinary or performance related issue, I would recommend phrasing any disciplinary allegation with reference to STPCD. For example, §50.16 could be particularly useful when dealing with an obstructive member of staff, refusing to communicate effectively with the senior leadership team and/or colleagues:

"50.16. Collaborate and work with colleagues and other relevant professionals within and beyond the school".

Burgundy and Green Books

Practitioners should be aware of both the Burgundy (for teaching staff) and Green (for others) Books; both of which represent the national collective agreement between the main trade unions and local authorities.

Burgundy Book: Notice Provisions

The Burgundy Book – to give it its full title, the Conditions of Service for School Teachers in England and Wales represents the national agreement between the main teaching unions and the local education authorities. It applies to all teaching staff in maintained Schools. In the case of an academy, those Employees who transferred on conversion will be covered by Burgundy Book terms and conditions as they existed at the time of the conversion. Any staff employed post-conversion will not be employed on Burgundy Book terms unless the academy expressly account for this within their contracts of employment. The full document runs to 68 pages; the most current version is as published in August 2000.

The Burgundy Book provides specific notice periods on dismissal or resignation, at paragraphs two & four. Paragraph two deals with payment details in the case of resignation; including the stipulation that those resigning ought to be paid up to the end of the term in which notice is given.

The notice requirements for either dismissal or resignation are as follows:

For teachers – a minimum of two months' notice, except for the Summer term where the minimum is three months' notice;

For Headteachers – a minimum on three months' notice, except for the Summer term where the minimum is four months' notice.

Any teacher with more than 8 years' service will benefit from the additional notice period specified by s.86 of the Employment Rights Act, i.e. one week for each year of service, up to a maximum of twelve weeks. The notice periods apply to all dismissals, for any reason other than gross misconduct.

Crucially, however, the notice period must be timed so as to terminate at the end of a school term; making the regime some-what restrictive.

School terms are defined for Burgundy Book purposes as follows:

- Summer: May 1st to August 31st;

- Autumn: September 1st to December 31st:

- Spring: January 1st to April 30th.

The notice periods set out in the Burgundy book create a number of potential issues to be aware of. Firstly, in the case of dismissal for matters falling short of gross misconduct, consideration as to the relevant timing of any notice needs to be considered: both in terms of payment in lieu (and both the STPCD and the Burgundy book are silent on the issue of payment in lieu) and in terms of the service of notice. This creates potential problems, as already seen in relation to the School Staffing (England) Regulations and the *Birmingham City Council v. Emery* case mentioned above. Secondly, the restrictive nature of the notice provisions can create recruitment problems also; giving Schools little time to recruit, particularly when staff members resign at the end of the Spring term.

Very often, simply the fact of the extensive notice periods can lead to Schools looking to conclude settlement agreements at the end of the Summer term as a means of avoiding, for example, lengthy performance management processes. In those circumstances, it is common for trade unions and/or their representatives to delay the negotiation in order to argue for a later termination date: and concomitantly more money for the member of staff in question.

Burgundy Book: Sickness and Maternity benefits

The Burgundy book sets out the provisions on sickness and maternity pay applying to teachers. On sick pay, the entitlement is as
follows:

During the first year of service	Full pay for 25 working days; after four months service half pay for 50 working days
During the second year of service	Full pay for 50 working days then half pay for 50 working days
During the third year of service	Full pay for 75 working days then half pay for 75 working days
From four years' plus	Full pay for 100 working days and half pay for 100 working days

Note that service for these purposes includes all employment as a
teacher with one or more local education authorities. Again, this is
a point that should be checked upon appointment. If a Teacher
goes from a maintained school to an academy, their entitlement is
effectively 'frozen', until such time as they enter into employment
in the maintained sector again (unless the academy in question
adopts the Burgundy book within their contracts of employment).
It is a matter for each individual academy to determine how they
will deal with sick leave entitlement, and whether they will honour
Burgundy book-style provisions for new starters: TUPE will
provide they will have to for any pre-conversion staff. There is a
discretion for individual employers to exceed the minimum entitlement for sick leave.

In relation to service-related maternity benefits, the same regime applies. The benefits are as follows:

First four weeks of absence	Full pay, offset against SMP
Next 2 weeks of absence	90% of salary, offset against SMP
Next 12 weeks	Half pay, without deductions unless SMP and half pay would exceed normal amount of full pay
Any further absence	Nil pay up to date of return

To be eligible, the Employee must have completed one years' service as a teacher within a local education authority. Those that do not meet this criterion are entitled to normal statutory maternity benefits. Furthermore, in the event the Employee does not return after maternity leave for at least thirteen weeks, they are to refund an amount determined by the Employer at the Employer's discretion. This does not include any elements relating to statutory maternity pay; and the Employer can also waive the requirement to return for thirteen weeks, or shorten it, again at their discretion. Note also that in calculating the thirteen-week period, periods of school closure are taken into account.

Green Book

The Green Book – to give it the full title, the National Joint Council for Local Government Services National Agreement on Pay and Conditions of Service – applies to all Employees in local government service. For our purposes, all non-teaching staff within a maintained School will be subject to Green Book terms and conditions. In the case of an academy, as with the Burgundy Book, those Employees who transferred on conversion will be covered by Green Book terms and conditions as they existed at the time of the conversion. Any staff employed post-conversion will not be employed on Green Book terms unless the academy expressly account for this within their contracts of employment. The full document runs to 222 pages, and it would be outside the scope of this work to summarise the whole.

Green book notice periods (for the Employer) mirror those of s.86 Employment Rights Act 1996 – i.e. one week for each year of service up to a maximum of 12 weeks. An Employee must give a minimum period of notice of the period from one pay period to the next – i.e. for monthly paid staff, one month.

In respect of service-related maternity pay benefits, the provisions mirror those of the Burgundy Book, set out above.

The entitlement to sick pay is as follows:

During the 1st year of service	One month's full pay, plus two months half pay once the Employee has completed four month's service
During 2nd year of service	Two months full pay and two months half pay
During 3rd year of service	Four months full pay and four months half pay
During the 4th and 5th year of service	Five months full pay and five months half pay
After 5 years' service	Six months full pay and six months half pay

Periods of sick pay can be extended at the discretion of the Employer in exceptional cases.

Independent Schools and Academies

Independent Schools have a free choice as to terms and conditions. Particular issues to be aware of are the provision of benefits which is commonplace in the Independent sector: particularly reduced fees for children of the Employee, and the provision of accommodation. Care should be taken in both cases to ensure correct drafting of such benefits from a tax perspective and in the event of termination: it would, for example, be wise to include repayment provisions within the Contract in the event of the staff member leaving midway through the term when their children have the benefit of free or reduced fee places at the School. It might be appropriate to consider 'good leaver' and 'bad leaver' clauses, similar to those seen in Directors' service agreements and shareholders' agreements in these circumstances. The effect there is to allow a staff member to leave without forfeiting the reduced fees in circumstances where the School deems them to be 'good leavers': one example might be in the event of the staff member being made redundant.

Commonly, Independent Schools will enjoy longer periods of leave; however, those with boarding facilities will often require comparatively unsociable hours of work. In the case of those staff with accommodation on or close to the premises in a school with boarding provision, it is sensible to include an opt-out from the 48-hour working week (as per Regulation 5 of the Working Time Regulations 1998).

Similarly, academies also have freedom of choice in respect to terms and conditions. In practice, most academies (at least initially) adopt STPCD – TUPE of course coming in to play; as we will discuss later. Note, however, that unless the academy agrees to subsequently adopt each new iteration of STPCD, the governing document will be the one that existed at the time of the transfer: following the decision in *Parkwood Leisure Ltd v. Alemo-Herron [2013] IRLR 744.*

Some academies take the approach of employing existing (i.e. pre-transfer) staff on STPCD, and new (i.e. post-transfer) staff on different terms and conditions. As more Schools become academies, the move away from STPCD is likely to become more prevalent, but this can create issues. Firstly, recruitment of staff on non-STPCD terms and conditions can be difficult. Secondly, there is the potential to create a two-tier workforce, which may also raise Equal Pay issues. Care should also be taken to avoid an unlawful inducement to forego collective bargaining rights, contrary to s.145B of the Trade Unions and Labour Relations

(Consolidation) Act 1992: as in *Kostal UK Limited v. Dunkley and others [UKEAT/0108/17/RN]* (which is discussed in more detail in the Chapter on Trade Union Relations).

Modification Order

The provisions of the Redundancy Payments (Continuity of Employment in Local Government etc.) (Modification) Order 1999, have the effect of preserving continuity of employment at least for redundancy payment purposes within the sector, and more generally between public sector bodies. The Modification Order lists the bodies to which it applies within the Schedules to the Order, and reference to this should be made in the case of any uncertainty. Section 3 to Schedule One deals with Education, and covers all maintained Schools, as well as further education colleges and universities.

Although it is not easy to spot, academies are covered by the Modification Order: specifically, at Schedule 1, Section 3: paragraph 8.

The effect of the Modification Order needs to be borne in mind when conducting a redundancy exercise, as this can significantly affect the costs involved; effectively increasing the amount of redundancy payment that might be due. Wherever a redundancy exercise is contemplated, it would be sensible to conduct due diligence of those employees potentially affected, in order to correctly ascertain the position.

The Modification Order does not, however, preserve continuity for unfair dismissal purposes - so although the Employee may be entitled to a redundancy payment, they will not be entitled to claim ordinary unfair dismissal unless they have attained the normal two years' period of service.

The Modification Order also applies to avoid the need to make a redundancy payment where an Employee takes up new employment with another Modification Order body either before termination, or within four weeks. Similarly, the provisions as to 'suitable alternative employment' apply as between Modification Order bodies: entitling an Employee to a statutory four-week trial period, and entitling an Employer to refuse to make a redundancy payment where an Employee unreasonably refuses suitable alternative employment. Although the suitability of alternative employment is viewed objectively, following *Readman v. Devon Primary Care Trust [2013] IRLR 878*, the Tribunal will assess the reasonableness of the Employee's refusal in light of their own personal circumstances; importing a degree of subjectivity. The decision to withhold a redundancy payment is therefore one to be taken carefully; following open and frank consultation with the affected employee in order to properly address the issue of suitability in light of the Employee's individual circumstances.

Pensions Issues: Generally

All staff employed within a maintained school, academy or further education college will be automatically eligible to enter either the Teachers' Pension Scheme or the Local Government Pension Scheme.

Both Schemes are underpinned by a vast statutory framework; but the principal Regulations most utilised by practitioners will be the Teachers Pensions Regulations 1999; and the Local Government Pension Scheme Regulations 2013.

For LGPS members, the Scheme is run by an 'administering authority' which is normally the local authority where the School is based. Academies must secure an admission agreement with the relevant administering authority in order to offer the Scheme: ordinarily this will be an uncontroversial part of the conversion process. TPS is administered by the Teachers' Pension Scheme Board.

Save for pension loss claims consequential upon loss of employment, disputes relating to pension will be in the jurisdiction of the Pensions Ombudsman: a route only open to individuals once all internal avenues have been exhausted.

In practice, I would recommend initial familiarisation with that part of the Regulations that deal with benefits: for TPS, Regulations 45-81; and for LGPS, Regulations 30 -52.

Ill-Health Benefits

Both Schemes provide generous ill-health retirement benefits provided certain criteria are met.

TPS is the simpler of the two, requiring that, to be eligible, the ability to work must be impaired by more than 90%, and likely to be so permanently. There is no entitlement if the member is on the 'barred list'; and the entitlement ceases upon the member entering into further employment as a teacher (but not in another role; for example, a teaching assistant).

Regulations 35 – 39 of the LGPS Regulations set out an entitlement to one of the three-tiers of benefit if the employment is terminated on the grounds of ill-health.

The specific tier a member will receive depends of their condition, its duration and its effect on their ability to undertake gainful employment.

The tiers are as follows:

Tier 1 – where the individual is unlikely to be capable of undertaking gainful employment before normal pension age;

Tier 2 – where the individual is not entitled to Tier 1 benefits, and is unlikely to be capable of undertaking gainful employment within three years of leaving employment; but is likely to be able to undertake gainful employment before reaching normal pension age; and

Tier 3 – where the individual is likely to be capable of undertaking gainful employment within 3 years of leaving employment (or before normal pension age if earlier) – in which case benefits will subsist until the individual obtains gainful employment.

'Gainful Employment' is defined as paid employment for not less than 30 hours a week in a period of not less than 12 months. Note that individuals in receipt of Tier 3 benefits may request a review by their employer for their entitlement to be reviewed (normally with a view to being placed on Tier 2). The relevant provision is Regulation 37. Although the Regulations import a suggestion of discretion on the part of the Employer (*"A Scheme Employer may..."*), in reality the Employer is likely to have to comply with this request. This can of course, create an extra liability for a School faced with such a request if they have to pay a further pension strain following an increase in the tier awarded: and the review request may come some time after the termination of employment (up to 3 years). Note also the Employer has an obligation to review the payment of Tier 3 benefits after 18 months of

them being paid: Regulation 37(5). This will involve obtaining a further certificate from an IRMP.

In all cases, it is necessary to obtain a report from an Independent Registered Medical Practitioner (IRMP) before an award is granted. Crucially, the Employer does have a decision-making role, although the Regulations provide little meaningful scope for disagreeing with the view of the IRMP. The authority of the person making the decision is a point to check, with reference to any Scheme of Delegation in place at the establishment in question.

In 2011, The Department for Communities and Local Government produced guidance on this area, which can be found on the excellent LGPS Regs website, www.lgpsregs.org. The Guidance must be borne in mind when advising on this area.

In both cases, there is normally a cost to the Employer (referred to as the 'pension strain'); a sum the Employer pays to the administering authority. This can be substantial.

Pension Issues: Restructuring

The pension strain can also become a problematic issue for the unwary when dealing restructuring and/or programmes of redundancy.

Both Schemes provide access to a pension payable without actuarial reduction to account for lost years in the event of termination by reason of redundancy or business efficiency; or where employment is termination by mutual consent on those grounds (I.e. Voluntary redundancy). This is subject to the Employee in question being aged 55 or over at the time of dismissal.

As both scenarios will create a pension strain payable by the Employee to the administering authority, this must be borne in mind as part of costing any redundancy exercise. It should also be borne in mind when drafting settlement agreements for all those aged 55 or over, whatever the reason for termination, in order that this issue is clear. Furthermore, if the Educational establishment outsources the payroll function, care should also be taken to ensure that the payroll provider notifies the administering authority of the correct reason for termination, to avoid an inadvertent payment of enhanced pension.

In extreme circumstances, it may be necessary to time the termination prior to an Employee attaining the age of 55, as in *Woodcock v. Cumbria Primary Care Trust [2012] IRLR 491, CA.*

In that case, Mr Woodcock (who at the time was Chief Executive of North Cumbria PCT) was served with 12 months' notice of redundancy when he was just short of his 49th birthday. No prior consultation had taken place with him. The reason for the timing of the notice was so that it expired, and his employment terminated, prior to him attaining the age of 50. The effect of that was that he was not therefore entitled to an enhancement of his pension on termination. Unsurprisingly, Mr Woodcock brought Tribunal proceedings alleging direct age discrimination, since, he alleged, any comparator would have been consulted with prior to notice being served.

The Trust relied on a justification argument to defeat the direct discrimination claim; namely that their treatment of Mr Woodcock amounted to a proportionate means of achieving a legitimate aim. Finding that consultation would in any event have been meaningless (the Claimant's evidence being that he would only have considered another Chief Executive role, and no such role being available); the legitimate aim being the aim of the Trust to bring Mr Woodcock's employment to an end without incurring cost to the taxpayer. The likely cost to the Employer of funding the enhanced pension (had he attained age 50) was estimated as at least £500,000.

Clearly, the facts in Woodcock are somewhat unique, but nevertheless serve as a useful example in the event of an extreme circumstance; together with a useful reminder of the need to be careful to check ages when planning any restructuring exercise involving Employees with the benefit of either TPS or LGPS.

Pension Loss Claims in Tribunal Litigation

Of course, the fact that either scheme is a generous final salary scheme imports further consideration in the event of Tribunal litigation, since pension loss will likely form one of the heads of claim. This is particularly the case if the litigation in question is unaffected by the 12-month cap imposed by s.124 Employment Rights Act 1996; and those advising Claimants in this area ought to consider the availability of those claims which can avoid the 52-week cap imposed by s.124; and/or the maximum compensation limit this imposes. In the case of an Employee with significant service, the pension loss claim can often exceed the loss of earnings claim – particularly if the complex loss calculation is used.

In August 2017, long overdue Presidential guidance on the principles the Tribunal ought to utilise in compensating pension loss was released. A copy can be obtained online. This Guidance makes greater use of the Ogden tables, and provides for different methods of calculation for both the simplified and substantial (now called complex) loss approach. The complex loss approach is at first glance a difficult calculation, but patient and careful use of the guidance should enable any practitioner to produce an accurate calculation without recourse to expert evidence except in those cases with significantly high value.

The real nub to consider is whether the Tribunal will adopt the simple or complex loss approach; since the outcome is significantly different financially. The Employment Appeals Tribunal considered this issue in an Education context in *Sibbit v. St Cuthbert's Catholic Primary School [2010] UKEAT 0070_10_2005*. In that case, the Claimant dismissed unfairly for gross misconduct on the 9th June 2008. She was due to retire in any event upon her 60th birthday, i.e. on the 31st August 2009. In awarding pension loss, the Tribunal at first instance determined the simplified loss approach was appropriate. The difference in question between the two calculations was relatively significant – approximately £4,000.00. The Claimant appealed, and HHJ McMullen, whilst accepting the calculation of compensation is normally a matter for the discretion of the Tribunal, found that the Tribunal had made an error of principle in not utilising the substantial loss approach. This was clearly the correct approach, in a situation where:

"the employment was of a stable nature; the Claimant had been employed for a considerable time, 23 years; she was unlikely to be affected by the economic cycle and she was less likely to be looking for new pastures" (HHJ McMullen, at § 22).

Although the Guidance has been updated, the principle is still sound. Clearly, the risk of a substantial pension loss claim will influence the advice given in the management of Tribunal litigation.

Summary

There are, therefore, a number of different sources to analyse and consider when advising on terms, conditions and wider contractual issues. A detailed understanding of this area is crucial to advising Schools; enabling practitioners to spot issues before they arise, and to accurately assess the costs and likely timescales involved in a particular course of action. Over time, it may be the case that STPCD, and the Burgundy and Green books become less important within the sector, as more Schools convert to academies and choose to utilise their own terms and conditions. However, that seems unlikely, particularly as STPCD and the Burgundy Book are seen by those in the teaching profession as the gold standard: any School or Academy that moves away from them wholesale may find themselves facing significant recruitment challenges. Similarly, although a move away from Teacher and Local Government Pension Schemes may seem financially attractive, this could again result in recruitment and retention issues given the valuable nature of the benefits prescribed under those Schemes.

CHAPTER THREE
SAFEGUARDING & DISQUALIFICATION
BY ASSOCIATION

Introduction

The safeguarding of children within their care is one of, if not the, most important duty of Schools. Safeguarding pervades all actions a School takes; and is perhaps the ultimate 'business case' when making difficult employment decisions. The law sets out specific safeguards Schools are required to undertake to comply with their statutory duty of safeguarding, and on any issue in this area, practitioners should have reference to the statutory DfE Guidance: *"Keeping Children Safe in Education"*. In this Chapter, we will look at DBS checks generally, and then focus on the Disqualification by Association regime.

DBS Checks Generally

Prior to employing staff, Schools are required to obtain an up to date certificate from the Disclosure and Barring Service; which will disclose criminal offences, and also information about whether the prospective employee is on the 'barred list' if an enhanced check is sought.

The statutory DfE Guidance 'Keeping Children Safe in Education' expects that most employees will need an enhanced check due to the likelihood of them engaging in regulated activity:

"87. The level of DBS certificate required, and whether a prohibition check is required, will depend on the role and duties

of an applicant to work in a school or college, as outlined in this guidance.

88. For most appointments, an enhanced DBS certificate, which includes barred list information, will be required as the majority of staff will be engaging in regulated activity. In summary, a person will be considered to be engaging in regulated activity if, as a result of their work, they:

• *will be responsible, on a regular basis in a school or college, for teaching, training instructing, caring for or supervising children; or*

• *will carry out paid, or unsupervised unpaid, work regularly in a school or college where that work provides an opportunity for contact with children; or*

• *engage in intimate or personal care or overnight activity, even if this happens only once."*

The Childcare (Disqualification) Regulations 2009 go further, preventing Employers from employing those involved in Early and Later Years (in practice under 8 year-olds) if that person is convicted of a relevant offence, or if they are on the 'barred list'. The DfE has produced statutory guidance on the Regulations - *"Disqualification under the Childcare Act 2006"* which applies to local authorities, maintained schools, academies and free schools.

A person will be included on the barred list if one or more of the following apply:

• The individual has been convicted or cautioned for sexual offences against children;

- They have been cautioned or convicted for other offences (kidnapping, murder, some sexual offences against an adult);

- They are subject to a risk of sexual harm order;

- They are subject to a disqualification order and the DBS has reason to believe they have been or might engage in regulated activity;

- They have engaged in relevant conduct – i.e. conduct which endangers or likely to endanger a child, conduct which would do so if repeated, conduct involving sexual material relating to children or inappropriate sexually explicit images depicting violence against human beings and inappropriate conduct of sexual nature involving a child;

- They satisfy the harm test – i.e. individual may harm a child, cause a child to be harmed, put a child at risk of harm, attempt to harm or incite another to harm a child.

In practice, Schools are unlikely to have employed those individuals; since those matters will have been disclosed upon obtaining the DBS certificate.

Remember that the 2009 Regulations only apply to those staff working within and Early Years and/or Foundation Stage settings. This includes both before and after school provisions (e.g. Breakfast clubs and the like). Staff within the following roles are not covered:

- Those who only provide education, childcare or supervised activity during school hours to children above reception age;

- Those who only provide childcare or supervised activities out of school hours for children who are aged 8 or over

Provided that those staff also have no involvement in the management of the provision. Schools are required to make their staff aware of the provisions of the legislation, and the guidance specifically makes it clear that they ought to be made aware of the disqualification by association provision set out in Regulation 9 (on which more below).

Disqualification by Association

Regulation 9 of the Childcare (Disqualification) Regulations prohibits the employment of a person who lives with someone who is on the barred list or who has been convicted of a relevant offence.

This Regulation, described as *'a draconian rule'* by Elias LJ, brings with it a number of practical problems when advising Schools. In particular, questions remain about the duty of disclosure upon a member of staff embarking upon a new relationship. Similarly, when is a person classed as living in the same household? Is it upon entry to the electoral roll? Or is it something looser?

In theory, one could argue that a teacher has a duty to inform the Employer should they become aware they are living with such a person, potentially as part of the duty of mutual trust and confidence, but whether this will happen is difficult to predict. Furthermore, an Employer is entitled to request this information from a staff member: whilst in the ordinary course of things requesting such personal information of a member of staff might not at first glance seem reasonable; due to the statutory obligation on Schools to safeguard those within their care, a Tribunal is likely to regard such a request as a reasonable management instruction.

Failure to follow a reasonable management instruction is a category of misconduct, and depending on the seriousness of the situation, can amount to gross misconduct. There are data protection issues to be mindful of; and §26 of the Childcare Act Guidance sets some parameters to be aware of:

- Schools should only ask those staff covered by the Regulations for the information (I.e. It is likely to be inappropriate or unreasonable to ask for this information from a member of staff not working within EYFS);

- The staff are only required to provide the information *"to the best of their knowledge"*;

- The individual to whom the information relates must be clearly informed about how and for what purpose the School will use the information;

- Schools must be certain that the information provided is adequate, accurate and relevant to their enquiries;

- Where information is provided in error, or is irrelevant, it must be destroyed.

Once disclosure is made, the Employer must take steps to ensure that member of staff is no longer employed in the early years' provision, or involved in the management of an early year's provision without a waiver being received: whether through paid leave or redeployment. Many will inevitably look to dismiss; conceivably the Employer could rely on statutory illegality, but many more will look to some other substantial reason as a reason for dismissal. A more detailed examination of some other substantial reason in an education context can be found in the chapter on Misconduct and Discipline.

A member of staff, if they are on the barred list, or the person they are associated with can make an application for a waiver via Ofsted. Schools are required to notify Ofsted upon becoming aware that an individual is disqualified; they must tell the individual that Ofsted has been informed, and the implications of the disqualification.

As referenced above, the Courts have dealt with the impact of these Regulations in *A v. B Local Authority and C Governing Body [2016] IRLR 779*. In that case, which concerned a maintained school, the head teacher was dismissed for failing to disclose her relationship with a man convicted of making indecent images of children. Although in the circumstances of the case the head teacher was not co-habiting with the man, the governors nevertheless dismissed her for gross misconduct; by reason of her failure to disclose the relationship. The School found that the fact of the relationship gave rise to a risk to the children, and that as a head teacher with safeguarding responsibilities she was under a duty to disclose the relationship. The Heads argument that this amounted to a breach of her Human Rights was unsuccessful; the courts regarding the disclosure of what would otherwise be a private matter to be necessary for the protection of children. Elias LJ, in a dissenting judgment, criticised the Disqualification Regulations in this way:

"I do not think that a draconian rule which disqualifies people from their jobs merely because of their association with offenders

should provide a basis for imposing other duties (in this case disclosure) on those who fall short of the necessary degree of association." (At § 50).

Summary

The rules on disqualification by association therefore create a number of potential issues to be aware of. Schools should consider the appropriate method of ensuring disclosure for affected employees; and consider appropriate mechanisms for regularly reminding those staff working within EYFS (or with management of that area) of their responsibilities. Consideration ought to be given to an appropriate policy or action plan to be implemented upon discovery of a member of staff becoming disqualified. It may not be as simple as an Employee embarking upon a new relationship, for example: it could cover Employee's parents – if they live at home – or their children. Theoretically, it could also apply to flatmates; although of course how far Employees would be expected to know of the offences and/or history of their flatmates will vary. The Regulations do not, in my view, go so far as obliging the Employee to make such enquiries for those with whom they co-habit; although as seen above, in the *A v. B* case, a School is probably entitled to take a stricter view in the case of senior leadership.

CHAPTER FOUR
MISCONDUCT AND DISCIPLINE

Introduction

In this chapter we will take an overview of some of the specific difficulties facing those advising Schools in misconduct cases. Bear in mind that when advising in this area on the employer side that it will be particularly unusual for an employee not to be represented by a Trade Union representative, since the sector is one of the most heavily unionised in the country. This rightly opens up any situation to particular, and potentially robust scrutiny; meaning care must be exercise far more than, for example, in dealing with misconduct by the Employee of an SME.

The points we will examine are as follows:

- Safeguarding and Suspension: with reference to the DFE's statutory guidance;

- Serious Case Reviews, DBS Referrals and Police Investigations;

- The role of 'Some other substantial reason' as a fair reason for dismissal;

- Children as witnesses in the investigatory process;

- The pitfalls to be aware of where governors are decision makers.

Suspension and Safeguarding

We have already seen the importance of safeguarding; and of course this becomes relevant to issues of misconduct on a regular basis.

Schools and Colleges must have regard to the statutory guidance issued by DfE, entitled *'Keeping Children Safe in Education'*. This document sets out specific rules for staff in dealing with safeguarding issues, and practitioners should familiarise themselves with it.

In particular, pages 40-51 provide useful guidance as to how to deal with allegations of abuse made against teachers and staff.

Early considerations will inevitably include the issues of suspension, referral to the local authority Social care services and/or the police. The Guidance requires that:

> *"It is essential that any allegation of abuse made against a teacher or other member of staff or volunteer in a school or college is dealt with very quickly, in a fair and consistent way that provides effective protection for the child and at the same time supports the person who is the subject of the allegation."*

Remember also that police involvement and suspension ought not be a knee-jerk reaction: see *Crawford v. Suffolk Mental Health Partnership NHS Trust [2012] IRLR 402*, a case which also highlights the care that ought to be taken before making a referral to the police:

"Footnote.

This case raises a matter which causes me some concern. It appears to be the almost automatic response of many employers to allegations of this kind to suspend the employees concerned, and to forbid them from contacting anyone, as soon as a complaint is made, and quite irrespective of the likelihood of the complaint being established. As Lady Justice Hale, as she was, pointed out in Gogay v Hertfordshire County Council [2000] IRLR 703, even where there is evidence supporting an investigation, that does not mean that suspension is automatically justified. It should not be a knee jerk reaction, and it will be a breach of the duty of trust and confidence towards the employee if it is. I appreciate that suspension is often said to be in the employee's best interests; but many employees would question that, and in my view they would often be right to do so. They will frequently feel belittled and demoralised by the total exclusion from work and the enforced removal from their work colleagues, many of whom will be friends. This can be psychologically very damaging. Even if they are subsequently cleared of the charges, the suspicions are likely to linger, not least I suspect because the suspension appears to add credence to them. It would be an interesting piece of social research to discover to what extent those conducting disciplinary hearings subconsciously start from the assumption that the employee suspended in this way is guilty and look for evidence to confirm it. It was partly to correct that danger that the courts have imposed an obligation on the employers to ensure that they focus as much on evidence which exculpates the employee as on that which inculpates him.

I am not suggesting that the decision to suspend in this case was a knee jerk reaction. The evidence about it, such as we have, suggests that there was some consideration given to that issue. I do, however, find it difficult to believe that the relevant body could have thought that there was any real risk of treatment of this kind being repeated, given that it had resulted in these charges. Moreover, I would expect the committee to have paid close attention to the unblemished service of the relevant staff when assessing future risk; and perhaps they did.

However, whatever the justification for the suspension, I confess that I do find it little short of astonishing that it could ever have been thought appropriate to refer this matter to the police. In my view it almost defies belief that anyone who gave proper consideration to all the circumstances of this case could have thought that they were under any obligation to take that step. I recognise that it is important that hospitals in this situation must be seen to be acting transparently and not concealing wrongdoing; but they also owe duties to their long serving staff, and defensive management responses which focus solely on their own interests do them little credit. Being under the cloud of possible criminal proceedings is a very heavy burden for an employee to face. Employers should not subject employees to that burden without the most careful consideration and a genuine and reasonable belief that the case, if established, might justify the epithet "criminal" being applied to the employee's conduct."

Clearly, therefore, this is a situation in which one must proceed with care. My experience dictates that many organisations will take a safety-first approach, and will in many circumstances suspend. Whatever the situation, I would always advocate a written notice being made of the decision, and the factors involved. It is worth noting that the Guidance suggests that suspension should not be the default position and an individual should be suspended only if there is no reasonable alternative. As set out in the opening chapter, the School Staffing (England)

Regulations govern who can suspend, and who can lift a suspension in the maintained sector. There are different rules dependent on whether the authority or the governing body is the employer; in both cases the governing body or the head can suspend staff, but *only* the governing body has the power to lift the suspension (albeit that the authority may also have this power, following the *Emery v Birmingham City Council* case). If the authority is the employer, they must be notified of the suspension immediately.

The High Court recently considered the suspension question in a School context in *Agoreyo v. London Borough of Lambeth [2017] EWHC 2019(QB)*; in which a decision taken to suspend amounted to a breach of the implied contractual term of mutual trust and confidence; and as such, a constructive dismissal. In that case, the Claimant was suspended 5 weeks after the commencement of her employment, allegedly because of the force she had used with two children in three separate incidents. The suspension took place against a background in which the Claimant had been in touch with the Head on numerous occasions requesting support for dealing with the children in question. There was no question that the School had to investigate the incidents – they did – but the question was whether it was reasonable and/or necessary to suspend the Claimant in order to conduct that investigation. Confirming (at § 24) the view that suspension is not a neutral act; in that case the suspension was regarded as largely a knee-jerk reaction, and as effectively the default position. That conclusion led to the finding that the suspension amounted to a constructive dismissal.

So, what practical advice can be given when determining whether or not to suspend? A non-exhaustive checklist would include the following:

• What is the type of School you are advising?

- Who has the power to suspend?

- What is the nature of the allegation?

- Does the allegation potentially require a DBS referral?

- Does it require a referral to the Local Authority Designated Officer and/or the police?

- What alternatives are there to suspension?

It would be sensible for the School to make a formal record of their decision-making process, addressing at a minimum the points listed above. Unless there are good reasons for not doing so, it would be sensible to set out the reasoning to the Employee within the correspondence confirming the suspension - this will certainly help to avoid an allegation of breach of mutual trust and confidence; and demonstrate that the suspension was not simply the default position of the School.

It is also worth considering whether the allegation itself could amount to a public interest disclosure; since in that circumstance care must be taken not to subject the 'whistleblower' to a detriment.

A final point to note is that the Education Act 2002 introduced reporting restrictions which prevent the publication of any material that may lead to the identification of a teacher who has been accused by, or on behalf of, a pupil from the same school. Confidentiality in these situations is therefore of the utmost importance; particularly in the age of social media where dissemination of information is both instantaneous and permanent.

Serious Case Reviews DBS Referrals and Criminal Investigation

Whenever an allegation involving safeguarding considerations is raised, Schools (normally the Head, or if the allegation is about the Head, the Chair of Governors) should consult with the Local Authority Designated Officer to agree a course of action. Dependent on the nature of the allegations, and any police investigation, the LADO is likely to convene a serious case review.

I have experience of the notes of a serious case review remaining confidential, and not being disclosed to those charged with investigating a potential disciplinary offence. This of course creates significant problems in both an internal disciplinary and any subsequent proceedings for unfair dismissal. It is important to establish the position with the relevant local authority and ensure that all parties are aware of this in advance of any disciplinary hearing to avoid any unfairness. Those representing the Employee may be able to make a subject access request to obtain the minutes; for the Employer if disclosure is not forthcoming the position is more difficult.

However, it is important to remember that the purpose of the serious case review, whilst arising from the employment is focused on entirely different issues to those an Employer is examining. For example, the fact that a serious case review may result in no further action does not mean that no disciplinary rules have been broken, and vice versa. The decision taken by the Local Authority Designated Officer, and for that matter the Police, is only of tangential relevance to a disciplinary situation. What is important is to ensure that all parties know the status of any notes of the serious case review, and get the same disclosure if it is forthcoming; and most importantly that the disciplinary process remains objective and independent of the outcome of either the serious case review or the police investigation.

The outcome of any allegation must be recorded in one of the following specific ways:

- Substantiated: there is sufficient evidence to prove the allegation;

- Malicious: there is sufficient evidence to disprove the allegation and there has been a deliberate act to deceive;

- False: there is sufficient evidence to disprove the allegation;

- Unsubstantiated: there is insufficient evidence to either prove or disprove the allegation. The term, therefore, does not imply guilt or innocence.

It is important to note that even in the event of a resignation or agreed severance, there will likely remain a duty on the Employer to make a referral to DBS and potentially the NCTL. This can cause barriers to reaching settlements in some circumstances, and I would advocate highlighting the position with the Employee and/or their Trade Union at the outset of any negotiations. The Keeping Children Safe Guidance warns against settlement in safeguarding cases; stating that it will not be appropriate to reach a settlement in the circumstances in which the criteria for a DBS referral are met. The Guidance also confirms that any settlement agreement that purports to prevent an Employer from making a DBS is likely to result in a criminal offence.

Paragraph 120 of the Guidance sets out the criteria for a referral to the DBS:

"Schools and colleges have a legal duty to refer to the DBS anyone who has harmed, or poses a risk of harm, to a child or vulnerable adult; where the harm test is satisfied in respect of

that individual; where the individual has received a caution or conviction for a relevant offence, or if there is reason to believe that the individual has committed a listed relevant offence; and that the individual has been removed from working (paid or unpaid) in regulated activity, or would have been removed had they not left."

The relevant statutory reference is the Safeguarding Vulnerable Groups Act 2006 (Prescribed Criteria and Miscellaneous Provisions) Regulations 2009 (UKSI 2009/37).

As a piece of statutory guidance, Schools and Colleges are required to comply with its provisions; the preamble to the Guidance confirm that the provisions should be followed unless there are exceptional circumstances. So where does this leave the question of a severance agreement in a safeguarding case? The answer is firstly that it will depend on the nature of the allegations and whether a DBS referral has taken place, or ought to take place. If it has, unless there are truly exceptional circumstances it would be prudent not to enter into a settlement agreement. If there is no referral, I would still advise caution. The safest course of action would be to conclude a detailed note of the business case for the severance agreement and the justification for it in each circumstance. The agreement ought also to be carefully drafted, making clear that a referral to DBS and/or NCTL can still be made. Similarly, any agreed reference must be carefully drafted; and in each situation I would advocate serious consideration to continuing with the investigation, which must in any event be concluded using one of the outcomes set out above.

Police investigations will inevitably have an impact on the internal investigatory process. Care must be taken to ensure that the internal investigation does not prejudice any criminal investigation. My practical experience dictates that the Police are aware of the need to conduct an internal investigation; and provided an open line of communication is maintained, and the steps you intend to take are made clear to the Police; they are often content for you to proceed. Of course, the pure time of any police investigation and subsequent criminal process can lead to delays in the process.

It is often suggested that a disciplinary hearing needs to be delayed until after criminal proceedings have been concluded. There is no rule of law to that effect (those in need of a case reference will find it in *Harris v. Courage (Eastern) [1982] ICR 530*); although the matter should certainly be considered with care.

This is particularly important if the Employee in question is in receipt of 'no comment' advice from their criminal lawyer. In those circumstances, those making the decision ought to be advised of exactly the purpose of a 'no comment' interview; and that it does not necessarily imply guilt. It is likely also in that circumstance that the Employee may be advised not to attend any disciplinary hearing for fear of self-incrimination. In that scenario, timing is important. A Tribunal is unlikely to find it reasonable for a disciplinary hearing to proceed shortly before, for example, a final hearing taking place in the criminal proceedings. I would always recommend checking the stage of any criminal proceedings before choosing to proceed with the disciplinary hearing, and making a detailed note as to the reasons why the hearing is going ahead, and the opportunities afforded to the Employee to attend (including the warnings given as to the matter proceeding in their absence in the event of non-attendance).

Referral to the Regulator

The National College of Teaching and Leadership is the regulatory body responsible for investigating allegations of serious misconduct against teachers and head teachers in schools in England. A referral can be made in the case of allegations of serious misconduct against a teacher; and can be made by:

- A teacher's employer (including a supply or employment agency);

- Members of the public

- The Police

- The Disclosure and Barring Service

A referral is only appropriate if the alleged misconduct is so serious that it warrants a decision on whether the teacher should be prevented from teaching. Schools have a statutory duty to refer to NCTL in all cases of serious professional misconduct; and must consider a referral whether there is a dismissal for misconduct, or where they would have dismissed but for a resignation by the teacher. Note that as this is a statutory obligation, Schools ought not to derogate from this responsibility, for example when concluding a settlement agreement.

NCTL have produced guidance on the factors they will take into account in making decisions leading to the prohibition of teachers from teaching; which Employers should utilise when deciding whether it is necessary to make a referral; if the Employer is in doubt a referral should be made. There are 3 factors that can lead to a referral:

- Unacceptable professional conduct

- Conduct that may bring the profession into disrepute

- Conviction of a relevant offence

The Guidance gives the following examples of what would normally be a relevant offence:

- violence;

- terrorism;

- intolerance and/or hatred on the grounds of race/religion or sexual orientation

- fraud or serious dishonesty;

- theft from a person or other serious theft

- possession of class A drugs;

- supplying of illegal substances of any classification;

- sexual activity;

- arson and other major criminal damage;

- serious driving offences, particularly those involving alcohol or drugs;

- serious offences involving alcohol;

- serious offences involving gambling;

- possession of prohibited firearms, knives or other weapons;

- any activity involving viewing, taking, making, possessing, distributing or publishing any indecent photograph or image or pseudo photograph or image of a child, or permitting any such activity, including one off incidents.

If a teacher has displayed behaviours associated with those offences, but have not been convicted, this is nevertheless likely to be unacceptable professional conduct: certainly if the Employee has accepted a caution.

The NCTL will normally await the conclusion of any internal process, and a Tribunal process if there is one, before making a decision. This can lead to potential difficulties in settling Tribunal litigation, since Claimants will naturally want the Employer to waive the referral to NCTL as part of the settlement, when this is not within their gift.

As there is potential for an internal process to ultimately lead to prohibition from the profession, it may in certain circumstances be appropriate for the Employee to be legally represented. In *R (G) v. Governors of X School [2011] UKSC 30*, the Supreme Court confirmed that the Employee in question ought to be afforded a right to legal representation in the internal process because there was the potential for the Employees Article 6 Human Rights to be infringed: due to the potential for his right to practice in the teaching profession being affected.[1] The facts of the case concerned a teaching assistant accused of sexual misconduct within a primary school.

If a School receives a request for an Employee to be legally repre-sented in these circumstances, the request ought certainly to be

---

1 Article 6 confirming "In the determination of his civil rights and obligations or of any criminal charge against him, everyone is entitled to a fair and public hearing within a reasonable time by an independent and impartial tribunal established by the law".

considered carefully; clearly the answer will be dependent upon the specific allegations in question. Furthermore, should there be the potential for a referral then the investigation itself will need to be treated sufficiently carefully: *Salford NHS Trust v. Roldan [2010 IRLR 721.*

Some Other Substantial Reason

In many situations, the use of 'some other substantial reason' can be considered as a reason for dismissal. Whilst this can be procedurally difficult – both in terms of the procedure one follows, and what is explained to the Employee – it can be a very useful tool for practitioners: providing a fair dismissal route when misconduct, for example, is difficult to prove in any satisfactory way.

Although it would be advisable to follow the principles of the ACAS Code wherever possible, *Phoenix House v. Stockman [2016] IRLR 848* is authority to confirm that the ACAS Code does not apply to SOSR dismissals.

Leach v. OFCOM [2012] IRLR 839 is among the leading cases in this area. In that case, OFCOM were notified that Mr Leach, employed by OFCOM as their International Policy Advisor (Professional Senior Associate) had been arrested in Cambodia on suspicion of child abuse offences. OFCOM has a statutory duty to have regard to the vulnerability of children. The advice from the Police was that they viewed Mr Leach as continuing to pose a threat to children. As a result of that, OFCOM took the decision, following a disciplinary hearing, to summarily dismiss the Claimant. The reason relied on was a breakdown on trust and confidence: reasoning that was criticised in particular by the Employment Appeals Tribunal.

In essence, however, the 'fair' reason for the purposes of s.98 of the Employment Rights Act 1996 was some other substantial reason. In these circumstances, the Court of Appeal agreed that OFCOM did have such reason for the dismissal of the Claimant. The factors that were especially relevant included the public reputation of OFCOM, the credible source of the information presented to OFCOM (the Police), and the efforts taken by OFCOM to balance the needs of the organisation against the potential for injustice to the Employee. Contrast that decision with the one reached in *Z v. A [2013] UKEAT 0203_13_0912*, in which the decision of a governing body of a primary school to dismiss a caretaker on the basis of information (again from the police) of an allegation of historical sex abuse was found to be unfair. In that case (which is also instructive of the difficulties facing a School where there is an ongoing police investigation), the School had demonstrated no sound basis for their conclusion that the Claimant posed a danger to children. The matter was still the subject of police investigation at the time of the dismissal; indeed at the time of the appeal, the Claimant provided a specific date for the conclusion of the police investigation which was only 8 days in the future.

Clearly, therefore, the situation must be approached with some caution. Taken from the OFCOM case, and paraphrasing, I would suggest considering the following steps when dealing with this type of dismissal:

1. The nature of the Respondent and the Claimant's role in it;

2. The nature of the allegations and the efforts made by the Respondent to obtain clarification and confirmation;

3. The response of the Claimant;

4. What alternative courses of action have been reasonably open to the Respondent.

In essence, it is a question of balancing the risk to the Employer as against the potential injustice to the affected Employee. Further guidance is provided in the headnote to OFCOM:

> *"an employer to whom a third party discloses information or makes allegations should assess for itself, as far as practicable the reliability of what it has been told, it should check the integrity of the informant body and the safeguards within its internal processes containing the accuracy of the information supplied. It should consider also the likely effect of disclosure and whether there was cogent evidence of a pressing need for disclosure to the employer."*

Anderson v. Chesterfield High School [2015] UK EAT 0206_14_1404 is a recent example of the EAT dealing with SOSR in a Schools context. In that case, the Claimant held a role at the School; which ceased upon him becoming Leader of Liverpool City Council. However, the employing authority (Sefton Borough Council) retained him as an employee on the basis that he would be paid the maximum allowed as paid leave to enable employees to hold public office[2]. This equated to approximately £4,500 per annum. The School subsequently became an academy, by which time the Claimant had become the elected Mayor of Liverpool, a role which carried with it an annual allowance to the tune of £80,000. Understandably, the Academy looked to terminate the employment of the Claimant, since the financial sum paid to him provided no benefit to pupils at the School. Although the procedure followed by the School was unfair, the reason –

---

2 s.10 Local Government and Housing Act 1989

some other substantial reason – was held to be a fair one in the circumstances.

The point about procedure raised in the *Anderson* case is a crucial one. Clearly, one wants to follow a fair procedure in order to avoid a finding of unfair dismissal, but what procedure should be followed? Should there be a procedure on 'some other substantial reason'? How would such a procedure be drafted, given the wide variance of factors that could fall under the remit of SOSR? The answer is not straightforward. As cited above, the *Phoenix House* case is authority that the ACAS Code does not apply to SOSR dismissals. I would advise following the procedure in place at the organisation that most closely fits that of dismissal with notice (any dismissal on SOSR grounds will of course be on notice). Often, this will be the disciplinary procedure; in which case care must be taken to ensure that the Employee properly understands the situation they are facing. Consideration should be given to proper explanation within the invite letter as to why the 'reason' relied on amounts to a substantial reason within the context of the organisation in question. It is akin to the formulation of a business case for redundancy/restructure that a business will go through prior to consultation. In that regard, reference to the Teachers' Standards requirements – discussed in more detail in the chapter on performance management – may assist.

It is also important that the decision maker has some under-standing of what is meant by some other substantial reason. Simply applying the moniker 'breakdown in trust and confidence' is unlikely to be enough for a Tribunal to accept: it is important to get behind why the reason is substantial for that particular School; and how it reasonably applies so as to justify the dismissal of the employee. Remember that the decision maker is likely to be cross-examined on this point; so a detailed understanding – which should be evidenced in the dismissal outcome letter – is crucial.

There is, of course, a temptation to simply rely on SOSR as an 'alternative' in pleadings. Whilst this of course is very common in redundancy situations (i.e. A business reorganisation falling short of redundancy); it should be adopted with caution in this scenario. Normally in this context, the situation is neither straightforward nor routine, and a Tribunal will expect a detailed explanation in order to properly balance any perceived or real injustice to the employee. Simply pleading SOSR as an alternative, without a detailed explanation, is unlikely to be successful (in my view) in front of a Tribunal Judge.

Children as Witnesses

Inevitably, in a disciplinary situation within a Schools setting, it is likely that the incident may either concern or have been witnessed by children. Gathering the necessary evidence from those children carries with it some challenges. Care should be taken to avoid collusion, and to avoid unnecessary leading: young children in particular may be prone to simply saying what they think is expected of them. When faced with this situation, consideration should be given to the following:

- Production of a method statement detailing the way in which the statement has been gathered;

- The setting of any meeting with the children – to make them as comfortable as possible;

- Taking the statements as soon as reasonably practicable;

- Consideration to inviting the Employee's trade union representative to any such meeting (although again, care needs to be taken not to unsettle the child);

- Making sure the statements are in the child's own words – if they can write them themselves, so much the better;

- Putting the welfare of the child first;

- Informing the child's parents of the need to produce a statement, and potentially inviting them to the meeting - as long as they themselves agree to maintain confidentiality, remembering that Schools have a statutory obligation not to publish information that could lead to the identification of a teacher who is the subject of an allegation by a pupil.

There is no easy way to approach this scenario: it is a difficult one, but following the steps above ought to make the situation as fair as possible. Further difficulties arise where the Employee wishes to challenge the evidence given by children (the ACAS Code gives them the right to); in that case the School must think carefully about properly balancing the needs of the children and the duty of care to the Employee. Whatever decision is reached will of course depend on the circumstances of the case – particularly the seriousness of the allegation – but a clear record of the decision reached, with an explanation of the reason why, ought to be made in each case.

A final point to note is the need to ensure the children's identity remain confidential in any Tribunal proceedings; since reporting restrictions in Employment Tribunal cases are only granted in extreme circumstances (normally cases involving disability, sexual misconduct or national security). This may lead to the redaction of names in statements; and certainly referral to the children as, say, Child 1, 2, 3 rather than names or initials is usually preferred by the Tribunal in my experience.

Governors as Decision Makers and the Role of HR

Very often in a Schools setting, the decision makers will at some stage be governors. This brings particular problems in advising in this situation; since those making the decision are generally volunteers without in-depth day-to-day involvement in the School.

Whilst that is good in terms of providing objectivity; without proper training and an understanding of the commitment involved it can be difficult to constitute a panel to hear a case of, for example, dismissal. My practical experience is that it can also lead to delays in the dismissal process whilst a panel is constituted.

In these circumstances, the role of HR advisors can be crucial; although care should be taken to ensure to avoid the errors found in *Ramphal v. Department of Transport [2015] IRLR 985*. This was a misconduct case arising out of an investigation in relation to the Claimant's expenses claim and use of hire cars. The HR advisor involved in the investigation, as well as advising on points of law and procedure, also commented on the level of culpability of the Claimant: so much so, that the investigation report went from advising a final written warning, to recommending dismissal. The EAT found the *'lobbying'* from HR to be unfair, and set out the parameters thus:

> "In my opinion, an Investigating Officer is entitled to call for advice from Human Resources; but Human Resources must be very careful to limit advice essentially to questions of law and procedure and process and to avoid straying into areas of culpa-

bility, let alone advising on what was the appropriate sanction as to appropriate findings of fact in relation to culpability insofar as the advice went beyond addressing issues of consistency. It was not for Human Resources to advise whether the finding should be one of simple misconduct or gross misconduct" (per HHJ Serota, at § 55).

In the *Ramphal* case, the investigating officer was inexperienced; and of course this is likely to be the case when a governor is appointed to conduct an investigation; or for that matter to chair a disciplinary or appeal hearing. It would always be sensible for refresher training to be provided in that situation, simply as part of diligent risk management. Just as the law requires a more careful investigation dependent on the seriousness of the allegation, and its potential consequences (Salford *Royal NHS Foundation Trust v. Roldan [2010] IRLR 721*), logic dictates that the care with which an employer ought to ensure those involved in the disciplinary process ought to be determined by the nature and potential consequences of the allegation.

Remember also that many of the institutions within the Education sector fall within the ambit of the Freedom of Information Act; and in any event experience dictates a greater use of subject access requests pursuant to the Data Protection Act by prospective Claimants: leading to the risk of HR advice being disclosed prior to proceedings; and of course it is not immune to an order for disclosure in an Employment Tribunal case in the same way that legal advice would be. This is perhaps especially the case with discrimination cases, particularly since the abolition of the questionnaire procedure.

Simply copying the legal team into correspondence, or marking such correspondence *'subject to legal privilege'* is not, of course, a complete solution; since the Tribunal (and the Information

Commissioner, for that matter) is entitled to take a view as to whether the communication properly attracts legal privilege.

A further point to be certain on is to ensure that the governors in question are as independent as possible in the process. Certainly, care should be taken as a minimum to isolate a section of governors from the issues, to enable them to conduct any potential appeal that may be forthcoming. For that reason, any reports to governors as part of routine gubernatorial business should be careful neither to prejudge the situation nor to refer in unnecessary detail to any ongoing investigation. I would suggest that it is dealt with as a private and confidential item on any meeting agenda.

It is often alleged that governor in question is 'tainted' in some way due to previous involvement with the employee in question. The allegation is essential the same as one of bias. With such an allegation, it is always a question for the individual governor themselves to address. It should not, however, be dismissed out of hand; and I would suggest that any allegation is dealt with within any disciplinary hearing and explicitly recorded both in the hearing minutes and in the outcome letter.

It may be the case, particularly in small School, that sufficiently independent governors are difficult to find: certainly the ones with sufficient spare time. In that case, within the maintained sector, it may be possible to co-opt governors for the hearing from another School within the authority. Similarly, in a multi-academy trust, governors from the local governing body may be available to deal with any hearing. The final resort would be the appointment of an independent person to chair any dismissal or appeal hearing. In any of those scenarios care should be taken from a governance perspective to ensure those chairing the hearing have been given the appropriate delegated authority and/or correctly co-opted to avoid any allegation that any subsequent decision has been made *ultra vires*.

Summary

As can be seen, advising Schools on any misconduct issue, but particularly one that may lead to dismissal, is something that should be approached with care. The Employee is likely to be represented by an experienced trade union representative; who certainly within the maintained sector is likely to be experienced in the procedures of the LEA in question. Furthermore, as teaching is at least a profession, and more likely a *vocation* as well, the impact of any dismissal on the Employee is likely to be extremely serious indeed; even more so if it results in a DBS referral and/or a referral to the regulatory body.

Those making the decisions may be inexperienced, and may be volunteers. What they are dealing with could well be vastly outside of their previous experience. Furthermore, there is always the temptation – particularly in safeguarding cases – for any potential allegation of harm to a child to lead to a blinkered, subjective approach from decision makers, who are, after all volunteering for a role as a governor primarily to further the interests of those children. Therefore, timely, robust and sensible advice is crucial to avoid unfair dismissals and adverse consequences.

CHAPTER FIVE
PERFORMANCE MANAGEMENT

Introduction

In this chapter, we will look at the subject of performance management with principal reference to the School Teachers Appraisal Regulations; which set out a statutory framework for performance related pay and appraisal. We will then look at particular problems areas in this context, and conclude with a look at sickness and ill-health cases within the sector.

School Teachers Appraisal Regulations

For teaching staff, performance management by means of appraisal is now underpinned by the statutory framework found in the Education (School Teachers' Appraisal) England Regulations 2012. Note these Regulations as drafted do not apply to Academies; but I would argue that any Academy that adopts STPCD as part of terms and conditions is bound to follow the Regulations.

This Regulation sets out specific requirements for the appraisal of teachers; linking this to pay progression as set out by paragraph 19 STPCD:

19. Pay progression linked to performance

19.1. The relevant body must consider annually whether or not to increase the salary of teachers who have completed a year of employment since the previous annual pay determination and, if so, to what salary within the relevant pay ranges set out in paragraphs 13, 14, 16 and 17.

19.2. The relevant body must decide how pay progression will be determined, subject to the following:

a) the decision whether or not to award pay progression must be related to the teacher's performance, as assessed through the school or authority's appraisal arrangements in accordance with the 2012 Regulations in England or the 2011 Regulations in Wales;

b) a recommendation on pay must be made in writing as part of the teacher's appraisal report, and in making its decision the relevant body must have regard to this recommendation;

c) where a teacher is not subject to either the 2012 or the 2011 Regulations, the relevant body must determine through what process the teacher's performance will be assessed and a pay recommendation made for the purposes of making its decision, except in the case of newly qualified teachers (NQTs), in respect of whom the relevant body must do so by means of the statutory induction process set out in the Education (Induction Arrangements for School Teachers) (England) Regulations 2012(7) or the Education (Induction Arrangements for School Teachers) (Wales) Regulations 2015(8);

d) pay decisions must be clearly attributable to the performance of the teacher in question;

e) continued good performance as defined by an individual school's pay policy should give a classroom or unqualified teacher an expectation of progression to the top of their respective pay range;

f) a decision may be made not to award progression whether or not the teacher is subject to capability proceedings.

19.3. The relevant body must set out clearly in the school's pay policy how pay progression will be determined, in accordance with paragraph 19.2.

The relevant body referred to will either be the Local Authority or the Governing Board, depending on who the Employer is; which is dependent on the type of School.

Judgment of a teachers standards is to be done by reference to Teachers Standards as set out by DFE from time to time. It is important to review the individual School/Local Authority/Trust policy (as the case may be) when advising on this area. The current Teachers Standards in relation to teaching are divided between teaching and personal and professional conduct. The teaching standards are as follows (preambled with the phrase *"A Teacher must"*):

- Set high expectations which inspire, motivate and challenge pupils

- Promote good process and outcomes by pupils

- Demonstrate good subject and curriculum knowledge

- Plan and teach well structured lessons

- Adapt teaching to the strengths and needs of all pupils

- Make accurate and productive use of assessment

- Manage behaviour effectively to ensure a good and safe learning environment

- Fulfil wider professional responsibilities

The personal and professional conduct requirements look principally at behaviours. The overarching principle is for teachers' to *"uphold public trust in the profession and maintain high standards of ethics and behaviour, within and outside school"*.

Problem Areas

There are some problem areas to be aware of. Logically, observation of lessons should form at least part of the mechanism for assessing a Teacher's performance; yet teaching unions are opposed to excessive observation; and for the most part insist on no more than 3 observations per academic year, totaling no more than 3 hours.

Apocryphal evidence also suggests that at least one teaching union is opposed to the use of numerical targets as part of the performance management cycle: so the setting of objective targets; and agreement thereon with affected employees and trade unions can be a difficult area. Indeed, when one looks at the Teacher's Standards, pure numerical assessment is self-evidently difficult; as indeed is any accurate assessment against what could be argued are quite subjective standards and goals.

Furthermore, in the case of governors making the decision, it is important that they have an understanding of their responsibilities (perhaps through training) and the role they pay in scrutinising the recommendations presented to them. Simply 'waving through' the recommendations given can create problems in the future; for example, if future performance issues are raised regarding the individual teacher.

Similarly, if there are outstanding grievance investigations this can also hinder the process. I would suggest wherever possible that consideration is given to the appointment of independent appraisers if there are 'live' grievances: although I appreciate this may not always be straightforward. Additionally, long term sickness cases will also present problems, particularly if the sickness is capable of amounting to a disability for Equality Act purposes.

In addition, many policies suggest that the appraisal cycle will not apply if an individual is undergoing performance management: but I would argue it is still important to ensure a pay review process and decision is undertaken.

The timescales involved also present practical problems. My experience dictates that teaching staff – whether at the coal face or part of the senior leadership team – are incredibly time poor. Whilst it is for each governing body to agree their own mechanism of appraisal, it is the accepted norm that the appraisal will have taken place by 31st October; which in practice means before the end of the first half-term. It is evident, therefore, that the temptation to simply fast track the pay decision without careful thought and proper scrutiny could certainly be significant; but this should be avoided for the reasons set out above.

Parental Leave Cases

Clearly, the appraisal of a teacher on long term parental leave may also prove problematic. Although s.13 (6) (b) of the Equality Act 2010 allows for special treatment to women in connection to pregnancy or childbirth, this should not be afforded without careful thought, as demonstrated in *Eversheds v. De Belin [2011] IRLR 448*. In that case, as part of a redundancy exercise, Eversheds applied a selection matrix which, amongst the factors included 'lock up', I.e. The length of time between completion of a piece of work and payment being received. Mr De Belin was in a pool with another solicitor, a female, who was on maternity leave at the time. Due to the maternity leave, her lock up could not be measured, so Eversheds decided to apply the maximum score for the criteria, leading to the redundancy of Mr De Belin. On appeal to the Employment Appeal Tribunal, the EAT held that Mr De Belin had been unfairly discriminated against; since the obligation to afford special treatment to women in these circumstances ought only to be such treatment as is reasonably necessary to compensate them for the disadvantage occasioned by the fact of their maternity leave. In this case, simply awarding the maximum score for lock up went over and above what was necessary.

By analogy, therefore, there is a real risk of discrimination if a School simply decides to award a pay increase for a woman on maternity leave, either by relying on s.13(6) (b) specifically, or simply waving the process. Similarly, not awarding a pay increase is itself likely to be an act of discrimination, self-evidently subjecting the woman to unfavourable treatment contrary to s.18 of the Equality Act, and for that matter s.74. The situation is clearly not straightforward. One view would be to treat the appraisal itself as a keeping in touch day; and to review the information and performance that is in place prior to the maternity leave, perhaps allowing some leeway for the fact that performance might be lower than expected due to the pregnancy. That would certainly go some way to providing special treatment, which must be the right thing to do, but without simply giving *carte blanche*. It is important that whatever solution is adopted, the member of staff in question is informed of the proposed process and how it will apply to her. Careful planning will certainly assist an Employer in this circumstance.

Capability Information

As cited previously, Regulation 8A of the School Staffing (England) Regulations 2009 requires governing bodies to provide information to new School employers (maintained or academies), on request, information as to whether the prospective employee has been the subject of capability procedures. This can be a particularly useful tool on recruitment; particularly where the reference received appears to be the subject of a settlement agreement. Similarly, those drafting settlement agreements within the sector should be careful to ensure that nothing in the agreement derogates from the statutory responsibility this Regulation imposes.

Furthermore, it self-evidently imposes an obligation on the Employer to retain these records: although this should be done carefully, particularly in light of the provisions set out in the forthcoming General Data Protection Regulation.

As a consequence of this provision, care should be taken before embarking on formal capability procedures, not least since this will potentially impact on the Employee's future employability prospects. *Salford NHS Foundation Trust v. Roldan* is authority than an Employer must take more care in an investigation the greater the potential consequences of a dismissal: there seems no logical reason as to why this would not extend to the decision to invoke capability procedures in a Schools context.

Sickness and Ill-Health

In January 2018, the Liberal Democrats published a response to their mass freedom of information request regarding sickness absence within the teaching profession for the year 2016-17.

Focused on England only, the highlights (if that is the correct term) revealed:

- 3,750 teachers are on long term leave for stress and mental health issues (a 5% increase on the year before);

- 1.3. Million days have been taken off by teachers for stress and mental health issues in the last four years;

- 312,00 days were taken off for stress and mental health reasons in 2016/17[1]

Clearly, the sector is one with a high incidence of sickness related absence; not just for stress, although of course that issue garners media attention. Management of sickness cases within the profession can be difficult, not least due to the regular breaks provided by school holidays.

Whilst the working time rules set out in STPCD are relatively prescriptive, teachers are expected to:

"work such reasonable additional hours as may be necessary to enable the effective discharge of the teacher's professional duties, including in particular planning and preparing courses and lessons; and assessing, monitoring, recording and reporting on the learning needs, progress and achievements of assigned pupils." (STPCD 2017, § 51.7)

Note however, that Governing Bodies and Head teachers have a duty to ensure a satisfactory work/life balance, and to adhere to the Working Time Regulations provisions (STPCD 2017, § 52.4). This is a point reinforced by the NASUWT in their

---

1 https://www.libdems.org.uk/3750-teachers-england-on-long-term-stress-leave

instructions on actions short of strike action, with the following instruction:

"Instruction 8: Members are instructed to refuse to implement any existing management-led policies and working practice which have not been workload impact assessed and agreed by the NASUWT"

Although the Teacher's Pension Scheme does have provision for retirement on ill-health grounds, the bar for attaining this benefit is set high: a teacher must demonstrate that their ability to work as a teacher is impaired by more than 90%, and is likely to be so permanently.

I would advocate that any sickness policy deals with short-term intermittent absences separately from long-term absences. As with any sickness case, thought should be given as to whether a disability for Equality Act purposes underlies the absence; with due consideration to reasonable adjustments.

Paragraph 19.9 of the Equality and Human Right Commission Code of Practice is particularly useful when considering this point:

*"Where an employer is considering the dismissal of a disabled worked for a reason relating to that worker's capability or conduct, they must consider whether any reasonable adjustments need to be made to the performance management or dismissal process which would help **improve the performance** of the worker or whether they could **transfer the worker to a suitable alternative role"**** (emphasis added).

When considering this guidance, it can be seen that simply extending trigger points, for example, within an absence management policy is unlikely to be a reasonable adjustment, certainly at the point of dismissal. Furthermore, the duty to make adjustments will only arise at the point at which the employee is certified fit to work if the adjustments are made, following *Doran v. Department for Work and Pensions UKEAT 0017/14*.

Note that the duty to consider transferring the worker to a suitable alternative role is likely to extend across the authority where the local authority is the Employer; and dependent on geographical location across the Trust in the case of a multi-academy trust.

In long-term sickness cases more generally, the decision in *BS v. Dundee City Council [2013] CSIH 91* helpfully sets out 3 factors to bear in mind before deciding to dismiss:

"First, in a case where an employee has been absent from work for some time owing to sickness, it is essential to consider the question of whether the employer can be expected to wait longer. Secondly, there is a need to consult the employee and taken his views into account. We would emphasise, however, that this is a factor than can operate both for an against dismissal. If the employee states that he is anxious to return to work as soon as he can and hope that he will be able to do so in the near future, that operates in his favour; if, on the other hand he states that we is no better and does not know, when he can return to work, that is a significant factor operating against him. Thirdly, there is a need to take steps to discover the employee's medical condition and his likely prognosis, but this merely requires the obtaining of proper medical advice; it does not require the employer to pursue detailed medical examination; all that the employer requires to do is to ensure that the correct question is asked and answered" (per Dorrian LJ, at §27).

It would seem sensible to address these points specifically within a dismissal outcome letter where practicable; not least to serve as an *aide-mémoire* in the event of Tribunal litigation.

Summary

Management of the performance of teachers within the sector is therefore a process that is not as straightforward as it would be for an ordinary employer. There are prescriptive guidelines to follow on appraisal; and care should be taken work with recognised trade unions throughout this process in order to avoid disputes.

Care also needs to be taken in the instigation of formal capability procedures; and absence management will also be a key consideration for those working in and advising the sector. As ever, the School year does not serve to afford significant time for the management of these processes; making forward planning and awareness amongst decision makers of crucial importance.

CHAPTER SIX
ACADEMIES & TUPE

Introduction

Nothing has changed the education sector as significantly as the move to academisation. Whilst government policy no longer seeks to force all schools to become academies, there has not been any diminution of the appetite to academies, certainly amongst successful schools. Whilst many Schools will choose to become academies, Schools do not always have the choice, since a School can be required to convert if one of three circumstances apply:

1. The School has received a warning notice from its local authority (normally this will concern education standards, health and safety, or a breakdown in discipline);

2. An Ofsted inspection has found that the School has "serious weaknesses";

3. An Ofsted inspection has found that the School requires "special measures"

In this chapter we will look at the different types of academy, the impact of TUPE and choice of terms and conditions open to academies, and concluding with an examination of some of the issues peculiar to multi-academy trusts.

Types of Academy

Academies can be either stand-alone, or form part of a multi-academy trust. Some academies may be 'empty-MATs' where they have set up the trust to run the MAT but do not have any Schools within the MAT.

The current trend from DfE is to encourage converter schools to either form, or become part of, a multi-academy trust. Single academies will only normally be approved if:

- The Schools latest Ofsted rating is at least good;

- The pupils' attainment and progress is high;

- The Schools' finances are healthy.

Single academies are nevertheless still required to support at least one other local school on conversion.

A MAT is normally constituted of an overall Trust body; with a Board of Trustees responsible for overall direction, delegating various functions to the local governing body of the individual schools to have control of. This 'loss of control' (whether perceived or actual) can be a barrier to Schools agreeing to become part of a MAT.

Sponsored academies are in place to support underperforming Schools as part of a multi-academy trust – which may be existing or set up. Sponsors obtain specific approval from DfE for this purpose.

Terms and Conditions and TUPE

Conversion to an academy will inevitably be a relevant transfer for the purposes of the Transfer of Undertakings (Protection of Employment) Regulations 2006.

Broadly speaking, academies are independent of local authority control and are free to set their own terms and conditions.

Practically, however, at least immediately post conversion, many academies will adopt STPCD and local authority policies and procedures (some of which may in any event have been contractual); and then move to their own documentation over time. STPCD is updated annually; as a creation of statute rather than the result of collective bargaining, academies have the choice as to whether to adopt each edition of STPCD: I would suggest that a formal decision to this effect is produced by the relevant governing body and/or sub-committee as appropriate.

The Burgundy and Green books (being national collective agreements) will also transfer as terms and conditions on conversion; but the academy is not necessarily bound by any future changes if they do not recognise the relevant unions. However, that is in practice unlikely to be the case.

The Academy, or the multi-academy trust (as the case may be) will be required to gain admitted body status for the purposes of being an Employer permitted to participate in the Local Government Pension Scheme. Prior to conversion, a valuation for the pension scheme will need to be obtained.

Whilst experience dictates that many conversions will be relatively harmonious; consideration should be given to ensuring appropriate consultation with those affected in line with Regulation 13

TUPE. Timing is an issue to be aware of here, not least since the award on a successful failure to consult claim to the Tribunal is up to 13 weeks' gross pay per affected employee.

There may be a degree of harmonisation upon joining a MAT: if there is consider carefully the availability of an economic, technical or organisation reason for any change. Similarly, conversion itself may be a trigger for restructuring and again this should be borne in mind as part of the conversion process; since this is at least likely to be a measure falling within the scope of consultation under Regulation 13.

The timing of the duty to consult, and when this is triggered, is something to consider carefully. Prior to receiving an academy order from DfE, Schools are required to consult with parents and relevant stakeholders. I would advocate that staff are informed at least prior to this stage as a matter of good industrial practice. The trigger for formal consultation in a redundancy context is normally when a decision is taken at board level. Applying that by analogy to an academy conversion, there is certainly an argument that consultation should commence once the governing body have taken the decision to convert. Certainly, the receipt of an academy order would trigger consultation; and in any event the consultation must take place long enough before the transfer to allow for meaningful consultation.

Multi-Academy Trusts

There are a growing number of emerging employment issues peculiar to multi-academy trusts. Significantly, ascertaining the correct Employing entity is an important starting point: it may be as simple as the Trust body itself, but complications could arise, for example, upon the amalgamation of two existing academies into one multi-academy trust.

There is also a temptation prior to bringing a School into a MAT for staff to be seconded to the 'target' school. In this situation it is important to ensure a secondment agreement is drawn up to set out clearly the terms and conditions of that secondment. This will also help to avoid an 'accidental' transfer; as in *Celtec Ltd v. Astley [2006] IRLR 635.* Although outside the scope of this text, thought should also be given to whether this secondment creates a VAT event through the supply of staff.

Consideration also should be given at an early stage to the make-up of the senior team within the MAT. The 'support team' element of any academy is potentially vulnerable to restructure here; since it may be that the newly-formed MAT is content with, say, one business manager overall.

Appointment of the Chief Executive of the MAT is also a key consideration. I would advocate careful thought as to whether, for example, an outstanding Head teacher is always the best candidate for the role of CEO: and similarly, bringing in someone from a non-educational background is also something to consider carefully. For the purposes of exercising its functions as an academy, information held by an academies proprietor is likely to be subject to the Freedom of Information Act. Therefore, the salaries of senior non-teaching staff could be subject to disclosure, so any justification arrived at in setting salary levels ought to be considered carefully.

Over time, there is clear potential for Equal Pay issues to develop within MATs: particularly where Schools join from differing Local Authorities. Furthermore, non-teaching staff joining a multi-academy trust from different authorities could well be employed on differing terms and conditions; so there may be a desire to move towards harmonisation. Again, thought will have to be given to ensuring there is an economic, technical or organisational reason for any change to avoid any TUPE-related complications.

I would advocate an equal pay audit at an early stage post-conversion; with regular review of this issue thereafter. This is particularly the case where the academy in question does not adopt a job evaluation scheme for non-teaching roles.

Inevitably, multi-academy trusts do provide opportunities for restructuring and business efficiency; by pooling resources for the support functions, and by the potential for collaboration of staff and leadership functions. This can, therefore, lead to the potential for restructuring. In this context, the normal rules on redundancy and restructuring familiar to employment practitioners will apply. Bear in mind, however, the potentially restrictive nature of the notice periods set out in the Burgundy Book, which will have an impact upon the process both in terms of length of time; and in terms of the duty to continue to look for alternative employment during the currency of the employment. This duty almost certainly will apply across all Schools within a Trust; although any role outside of the School in which the individual concerned is employed may not necessarily amount to a suitable alternative role avoiding the need to make a redundancy payment, particularly following the decision in *Readman v. Devon Primary Care Trust [2013] EWCA Civ 1110*. Thought should also be given as to whether any redundancy will trigger a pension strain to the Employer, as discussed in the *'Pensions Issues'* section above.

Summary

Although the government has dropped its pledge for every school to become an academy by 2022, nevertheless the number of schools converting to academies and/or joining multi-academy trusts continues to rise. Over time, this has the potential to lead to significant changes in the sector; particularly in divergence in terms, conditions, benefits and rewards; as well as the relationship that these organisations will have with Trade Unions. As we have seen, there are some specifics to be mindful of when advising an academy; however, the relative autonomy these organisations enjoy can on the whole lead to faster decision making, and the potential for a more dynamic approach.

CHAPTER SEVEN
TRADE UNION RELATIONS

Introduction

Education is the most unionised sector in the country; with 48% of staff being members of recognised trade unions. We have already seen the effect Trade Unions can have on the efficacy of management within educational establishments. It is certainly my experience that trade unions in this sector are amongst the most active; and, at times, militant. In this chapter we will look at the following:

- The changes brought in by the Trade Union Act 2016

- Facility Time

- Action short of strike action

- Disciplinary Action and Trade Union representatives

- The Right to be Accompanied

- Inducements away from collective bargaining

- Bargaining Units and local collective agreements.

Trade Union Act 2016

The Trade Union Act 2016 dramatically changes the landscape for any trade unions. In force on the 1st March 2017; some key changes to be aware of are:

- Ballot thresholds are now increased to a 50% turnout;

- The ballot paper must set out the nature of the issues, the type of action called for and the time period for such action;

- The voting paper must include a more detailed description of the dispute and the proposed action;

- Unions are required to give 2 weeks' notice of industrial action (although both parties can by agreement lower this to 7 days);

- The mandate will be taken to have expired within 6 months of the date of the ballot; or no longer than 9 months where agreed by the union and the employer;

- Unions must appoint a picketing supervisor;

- The power to introduce Regulations to control the cost of facility time within the public sector: we have seen the first of these with The Trade Union (Facility Time Publication Requirements) Regulations 2017.

It is too early at this stage to accurately assess the impact of the Act; but undoubtedly it will make formal industrial action harder to get off the ground. My team has seen a marked increase in union activity recently: whether this is just coincidence or a move to appear more relevant in the eyes of trade union members is a point of debate.

Facility Time

Facility time is the time agreed between an employer and a recognised trade union that is granted to individual representatives to enable them to carry out their trade union role. The legislative background is set out in ss.168 – 173 of the Trade Union and Labour Relations (Consolidation) Act 1992.

The Trade Union (Facility Time Publication Requirements) Regulations 2017, which came into force on the 1st April 2017, require maintained schools and academies with more than 49 full-time equivalent employees to publish on their website relating to facility time, by answering the following questions:

1. What was the total number of your employees who were relevant union officials during the relevant period?

2. How many of your employees who were relevant union officials employed during the relevant period spent a) 0%, b) 1% - 50%, c) 51%-99% or d) 100% of their working hours on facility time?

3. Provide the percentage of your total pay bills spent on paying employees who were relevant union officials for facility time during the relevant period.

4. As a percentage of total paid facility time hours, how many hours were spent by employees who were relevant union officials during the relevant period on paid trade union activities?

The relevant period is 12 months from the 1st April, and began on the 1st April 2017: publication must be done before the 31st July. It is logical to expect increased media scrutiny on the facility time and its costs once publication commences; and practitioners should take steps to ensure those they advise are prepared for the requirements of the Regulations.

Documentation of the actual facility time agreement can on occasion be problematic and a source of dispute: particularly where the agreement is long-standing. Any arrangement should certainly from part of due diligence prior to an academy conversion.

The DfE has produced guidance on the managing of facility time in maintained schools and academies. This non-statutory guidance provides parameters as to what DFE regards as a 'reasonable' amount of time off for trade union activities; and confirmed their view that no teacher funded by the taxpayer should work full time on union work. DFE also expects all trade union representatives to spend the majority of their working hours carrying out their school-based jobs. As we saw in the *Davies v. Haringey* case (cited in the *"Who is the Employer"* chapter), that is not necessarily the case on the ground.

The Guidance also recommends consideration of the following points when receiving a request for facility time:

> "• *Can the school accommodate the amount of time requested, and ensure adequate cover for safety and the provision of educational services?*

> • *Does the request contain the right information (e.g. purpose, time and place - including agendas of meetings where appropriate), and has enough advance notice been given to provide alternative cover arrangements where necessary?*

- *Does it attract paid or unpaid time (i.e. will the time be used to undertake specific trade union duties, or for activities which should not attract paid time off)?*

- *If the request cannot be accommodated is there a reasonable alternative?"*

Obviously, further thought may be given by the School as a result of the new publication requirements. As standard, wherever a request is refused or accepted, either the reasons why or (as the case may be) the specific arrangements agreed to ought to be recorded in writing.

Action Short of Strike Action

The NASUWT are currently asking their members to participate in action short of strike action. Formerly, the NUT – now the National Education Union[1] – was also instructing its members to participate in this action. The NEU has not held a ballot on action short of strike action since its formation, so those teachers ought not to still be participating in the action; although the NEU does regard the changes made as part of action short of strike action to be permanent changes[2] to working practices.

Those advising Schools with NASUWT cohorts should familiarise themselves with the relevant instruction/guidance. Both are stated to apply to academies as well as maintained schools, regardless of whether the academy in question has adopted STPCD.

---

1 The NEU came into being on the 1st September 2017, following a merger between the National Union of Teachers and the Association of Teachers and Lecturers

2 https://neu.org.uk/sites/neu.org.uk/files/NEU201_Tackling_workload_together_2 017.pdf

By way of example, returning back to our theme of appraisal, the NASUWT's guidance can be restrictive:

"Instruction 1: Members are instructed not to participate in any appraisal/performance management process which does not conform to all elements of the NASUWT appraisal/performance management checklist and the classroom observation protocol.

Instruction 2: Members are instructed not to participate in any form of management-led classroom observation in any school which refuses to operate a policy of a limit of a total of three observations for all purposes within a total time of up to three hours per year."

Strike Action

In the event of a successful ballot for strike action, an early consideration will be the potential for injunctive relief to prevent that action. Whilst of course possible in the relevant circumstances, further negotiation is always preferable to try and resolve the dispute. I would always advocate attempting to utilise the services of ACAS if appropriate; not least due to the potential for adverse publicity as well as the obvious detrimental impact upon pupils at the School.

Should a strike prove inevitable, it is important to control the situation. Although the union are now required to provide a picket supervisor, nevertheless I would advocate clear instructions to staff about their right not to be deterred from crossing a picket line; together with appropriate arrangements for staff who feel unable to cross the line. Worthy of note also is to ensure the correct deduction of pay for strike action (1/365), as confirmed by the Supreme Court in *Hartley and Ors v. King Edward VI College*

[2017] UKSC 39. Strike days do not count as pensionable service for either the Teacher's Pension or the Local Government Pensions Schemes.

The DfE have produced non-statutory guidance on handling strike action in Schools. This makes it clear that the Head teacher must take steps to ensure that the School must remain open for as many schools as reasonably possible. The decision on whether to open the School will be one for the Head teacher; save in Academy trusts where the decision falls to the trust, albeit that in most cases the decision-making power will be delegated to the Head. Head teachers, in line with the guidance, are entitled to ask staff member whether intend to strike; although staff could choose not to answer that question. Whilst a Head may ask other teachers to cover for strike action, staff cannot be compelled to provide cover: §52.7 STPCD:

> *"Teachers should be required to provide cover in accordance with paragraph 50.7 only rarely, and only in circumstances that are not foreseeable"*

By the very nature of the strike ballot, the need for cover is of course likely to be foreseeable. On cover generally, the position of the NASUWT, for example, is straightforward:

> *"Instruction 20: Members should refuse to cover for absence"*[3]

Maintained Schools and those academies set up prior to 29 July 2012 are covered by the provisions of the Specified Work Regulations 2012; which require that only qualified teachers may teach classes. Free schools and academies set up after that date are not bound by this requirement; although of course if cover is provided by non-qualified teachers or support staff in the event of a strike,

---

3 NASUWT National Action Short of Strike Action Instructions - Phase 5

one could imagine this to be a point utilised by the trade union in the inevitable publicity surrounding strike action. If the Head is on strike, they need to delegate their duties to another member of staff in accordance with Guidance. Note, however, that some duties of a Head are non-delegable: see §54 onwards in STPCD.

Disciplinary Action and Trade Union Representatives

Handling disciplinary matters involving trade union representatives is a careful matter. The ACAS code advises the following (para. 30):

> *"Where disciplinary action is being considered against an employee who is a trade union representative the normal disciplinary procedure should be followed. Depending on the circumstances, however, it is advisable to discuss the matter at an early stage with an official employed by the union, after obtaining the employee's agreement."*

It is common also to notify the regional representative prior to the suspension of an employed trade union representative. Of course, care must be taken not to be seen to be subjecting the representative to a detriment on the grounds of trade union activities contrary to s.146 TULR(C)A 1992. It is occasionally argued that suspension of a trade union representative amounts to a detriment on grounds related to union membership or activities. Clearly, this will depend on the circumstances of each individual case.

The Tribunal will be concerned with the *purpose* of the act in question (i.e. The suspension), rather than its *effect*: *Gallagher v. The Department of Transport [1994] IRLR 231, CA*. The burden of proof will be on the Employer to demonstrate the purpose of the act in question; it is important therefore to be careful before taking the decision to suspend. Further guidance on the decision to suspend can be found in the Chapter on Misconduct and Discipline. Many organisations will have separate sections of their disciplinary policy devoted to disciplinary situations involving trade union representatives, so regard must be had to those where relevant.

The Right to Be Accompanied – s.10 Employment Relations Act 1999

S.10 of the Employee Relations Act provides Employees with the right to be accompanied by a work colleague or a trade union representative at a disciplinary or grievance hearing. Should the work colleague or trade union representative be unavailable for the hearing, they have a right to request an adjournment provided the Employee proposes a reasonable alternative time within five working days. If that is the case, the Employer must postpone the hearing to the time proposed. Failure to comply with the provisions of s.10 gives rise to a potential Tribunal claim, for which the award is two weeks' pay, subject to the extant statutory maximum on week's pay.

It is the request to be accompanied which must be reasonable, and *not* the choice of companion: *Toal v. GB Oils Ltd [2013] IRLR 696*. It is difficult to envisage a situation in which a request to be accompanied per se would not be reasonable.

Normal practice in the sector is to try to agree proposed dates for such hearings with the Employee and/or their representatives in advance; and whilst that is desirable that can lead to delay, for example, when a specific representative is not available. Since delay in progressing such matters has the real potential to disadvantage both Employer and Employee (particularly when one bears in mind the recent case law on suspension and whether this is a neutral act), Schools should consider being prescriptive as to the timings of hearings; attendance at which, provided they are during normal working hours, can reasonably be regarded as a reasonable management instruction. This is particularly the case given the right to request a postponement. Occasionally Unions will threaten to invoke the postponement provision of s.10, without actually doing so. I would advise taking a hard line (within reasonable parameters) if in receipt of such communication, for the following reasons:

1. It is in neither parties' interests for the matter to be unduly delayed;

2. It is the Employee's right to request a postponement, not the Unions (although they can certainly act on the Employee's behalf); and

3. Nothing in the legislation affords the Employee the right to be accompanied by a specific trade union representative, just one that meets the definition of a representative within ss. 1, 119 of the Trade Union and Labour Relations (Consolidation) Act 1992.

All the main teaching unions ought to be sufficiently resourced to be able to provide a representative with the relatively generous time periods that most Schools provide when scheduling a disciplinary hearing.

Inducements Away From Collective Bargaining

In December 2017, the first decision on the correct interpretation and reach of s.145B of the Trade Union and Labour Relation (Consolidation) Act 1992 was produced: *Kostal UK Limited v. Dunkley & Others UKEAT/0108/17/RN*. For those unfamiliar with the provision, s.145B prohibits unlawful inducements which have the sole or main purpose of moving away from collective bargaining. In the <u>Kostal</u> case, the Employer was in pay negotiations with Unite. The Employers proposal was rejected on a ballot, leading the Employer to take the step of publishing a notice on notice boards in the workplace, setting out the proposed offer, and the fact that it had been rejected by the Unite ballot. The offer also incorporated a concomitant change to terms and conditions. Crucially, the notice continued by giving individual employees the opportunity to accept the offer individually: with the caveat that if signed agreement was not forthcoming by the 18th December 2015 (9 days after the notice had been posted); the Christmas bonus would not be paid. That communication was also confirmed in writing to the individual employees. The Tribunal and the EAT found this to be an unlawful inducement, and made the award prescribed by statute of £3,800 per employee, per inducement: a liability totaling in excess of £400,000 for Kostal.

Two things arise from this when advising the sector. Firstly, the fact that we now have appellate authority on the scope of s.145B may lead to more claims under this header. Secondly, those that are advising on changes to terms and conditions (for example, during a restructure or following a TUPE transfer) will need to tread carefully, particularly where termination and re-engagement is proposed as an alternative, or end point, where agreement cannot be reached.

Bargaining Units and Local Agreements

As the sector moves towards ever increasing academisation, it may be that the larger MATs seek local collective agreements with the recognised trade unions. Bear in mind the recent decision in *Lidl v. CAC [2017] EWCA Civ 328* on the scope of bargaining units; in which the Central Arbitration Committee recognised a bargaining unit forming just 1.2% of the Employer's workforce: Lidl's judicial review against this decision was unsuccessful. Clearly therefore, if there are sections of the workforce potentially not covered by any collective agreement (and there is potential for this in academies and independent schools), there may be an appetite on the part of the unions to push for formal recognition.

Summary

Trade Union relations remain a key consideration for those advising in the sector. Good trade union relations, and quality representation can be significantly beneficial to Schools; but conversely when relations deteriorate this has a significant impact on the organisation. Although the Trade Union Act 2016 has limited the situations in which strike action can be taken, the power of the unions and the role they play within the sector means that any situation must be handled with reference to the impact on any recognised trade unions. It should always be borne in mind that trade unions have significant resources, and will often fund litigation for their members; which again may have an impact on the advice provided to Schools.

CHAPTER EIGHT
USEFUL SOURCES OF
INFORMATION

I set out here my 'go to' sources of information when advising in the sector; particularly the web or other resources that I and my team utilise on a daily basis:

- STPCD – updated annually:
  https://www.gov.uk/government/uploads/attachment_data/file/636389/School_teachers_pay_and_conditions_document_2017.pdf

- LGPS issues – the current version is available at: http://www.lgpsregs.org. This provides an easily searchable version of the current regulations; access to the old regulations, as well as relevant guidance.

- Pension loss compensation Guidelines:
  https://www.judiciary.gov.uk/wp-content/uploads/2013/08/presidential-guidance-pension-loss-20170810.pdf
  (Admittedly, maybe not a daily used resource)

- DFE Guidance – *"Keeping Children Safe in Education"* :
  https://www.gov.uk/government/uploads/system/uploads/attachment_data/file/550511/Keeping_children_safe_in_education.pdf

- OFSTED Reports – particularly useful in checking the type of School in question:
  https://reports.ofsted.gov.uk

- Teachers' Standards – one page overview:
  https://www.gov.uk/government/uploads/system/uploads/attachment_data/file/665522/Teachers_standard_information.pdf

- Disqualification under the Childcare Act 2006 – statutory guidance:
  https://www.gov.uk/government/uploads/system/uploads/attachment_data/file/528473/Disqualification_under_the_childcare_act_June2016.pdf

- DFE Guidance – *"Advice on trade union facility time in schools'"*:
  https://www.gov.uk/government/uploads/system/uploads/attachment_data/file/410276/advice_on_trade_union_facility_time_in_schools_090315.pdf

- NASUWT Guidance – *"National Action Short of Strike Action"*:
  https://www.nasuwt.org.uk/uploads/assets/uploaded/b7ec630c-edcc-4b29-b449c86481bb60cd.pdf

- DFE Guidance – *"Handling Strike Action in Schools"*:
  https://www.gov.uk/government/uploads/system/uploads/attachment_data/file/553757/advice_on_handling_strike_action_update_September_2016.pdf

- NCTL Guidance – *"Teacher Misconduct: The prohibition of teachers"*:
  https://www.gov.uk/government/uploads/system/uploads/attachment_data/file/495028/Teacher_Misconduct_The_Prohibition_of_Teachers_advice_updated_26_Jan_2016.pdf

MORE BOOKS BY
LAW BRIEF PUBLISHING

A selection of our other titles available now:

'A Practical Guide to the 2018 Jackson Personal Injury and Costs Reforms' by Andrew Mckie
'A Guide to Consent in Clinical Negligence Post-Montgomery' by Lauren Sutherland QC
'A Practical Guide to Running Housing Disrepair and Cavity Wall Claims: 2nd Edition' by Andrew Mckie & Ian Skeate
'A Practical Guide to the General Data Protection Regulation (GDPR)' by Keith Markham
'A Practical Guide to Digital and Social Media Law for Lawyers' by Sherree Westell
'A Practical Guide to Holiday Sickness Claims, 2nd Edition' by Andrew Mckie & Ian Skeate
'A Practical Guide to Inheritance Act Claims by Adult Children Post-Ilott v Blue Cross' by Sheila Hamilton Macdonald
'A Practical Guide to Elderly Law' by Justin Patten
'Arguments and Tactics for Personal Injury and Clinical Negligence Claims' by Dorian Williams
'A Practical Guide to QOCS and Fundamental Dishonesty' by James Bentley
'A Practical Guide to Drone Law' by Rufus Ballaster, Andrew Firman, Eleanor Clot

'Practical Mediation: A Guide for Mediators, Advocates, Advisers, Lawyers, and Students in Civil, Commercial, Business, Property, Workplace, and Employment Cases' by Jonathan Dingle with John Sephton

'Practical Horse Law: A Guide for Owners and Riders' by Brenda Gilligan

'A Comparative Guide to Standard Form Construction and Engineering Contracts' by Jon Close

'A Practical Guide to Compliance for Personal Injury Firms Working With Claims Management Companies' by Paul Bennett

'A Practical Guide to the Landlord and Tenant Act 1954: Commercial Tenancies' by Richard Hayes & David Sawtell

'A Practical Guide to Personal Injury Claims Involving Animals' by Jonathan Hand

'A Practical Guide to Psychiatric Claims in Personal Injury' by Liam Ryan

'Introduction to the Law of Community Care in England and Wales' by Alan Robinson

'A Practical Guide to Dog Law for Owners and Others' by Andrea Pitt

'Ellis and Kevan on Credit Hire, 5th Edition' by Aidan Ellis & Tim Kevan

'RTA Allegations of Fraud in a Post-Jackson Era: The Handbook, 2nd Edition' by Andrew Mckie

'RTA Personal Injury Claims: A Practical Guide Post-Jackson' by Andrew Mckie

'On Experts: CPR35 for Lawyers and Experts' by David Boyle

'The No Nonsense Solicitors' Practice: A Guide To Running Your Firm' by Bettina Brueggemann

'Baby Steps: A Guide to Maternity Leave and Maternity Pay' by Leah Waller

'The Queen's Counsel Lawyer's Omnibus: 20 Years of Cartoons from the Times 1993-2013' by Alex Steuart Williams

These books and more are available to order online direct from the publisher at www.lawbriefpublishing.com, where you can also read free sample chapters. For any queries, contact us on 0844 587 2383 or mail@lawbriefpublishing.com.

Our books are also usually in stock at www.amazon.co.uk with free next day delivery for Prime members, and at good legal bookshops such as Hammicks and Wildy & Sons.

We are regularly launching new books in our series of practical day-to-day practitioners' guides. Visit our website and join our free newsletter to be kept informed and to receive special offers, free chapters, etc.

You can also follow us on Twitter at: www.twitter.com/lawbriefpub.